THE
SOFT ANSWER

VERBAL T'AI CHI
for Sociable Self-Defense

THE SOFT ANSWER

VERBAL T'AI CHI FOR SOCIABLE SELF DEFENSE

SUSAN LOWELL DE SOLÓRZANO

KATHRYN LYDON   MONICA SCHOETTLER

RITA SOLÓRZANO

SASSAFRAS BRANCHES, LLC

The Soft Answer Verbal T'ai Chi is a trademark of Sassafras Branches, LLC
Published by Sassafras Branches, LLC
Washington, DC
First Edition
Library of Congress Control Number: 2016920627
ISBN: 13: 978-0-9983851-0-5 (Paperback edition)

TheSoftAnswer.com

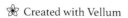 Created with Vellum

With deep gratitude to our families, for all their inspiration and support, and to Suzette Haden Elgin, on whose shoulders we proudly stand.

CONTENTS

INTRODUCTION

Virtually everyone has been on the receiving end of verbal aggression. It may have been in the form of an outright criticism, a backhanded compliment, a manipulative remark, or a socially awkward attempt at connecting. It may have sounded like one of these:

- *I love the way you just wear whatever you like, no matter what fashion dictates.*
- *Can't you do anything right?*
- *What's THAT supposed to mean?*
- *Even YOU should be able to understand this.*
- *Are you sure you want that cookie? Swimsuit season is coming up.*
- *It's just like you to declare the rules for everyone else.*
- *I had no idea you were that smart!*
- *Don't you WANT me to be happy?*
- *You need to smile more.*

A verbal attack may come at us from out of the blue, bubbling up in the middle of a conversation (or argument) with coworkers or family members. Regardless of where it comes from, it can leave us feeling frustrated, angry, hurt or speechless.

What can we do in the face of this kind of affront? So often, when faced with verbal aggression, we might be inclined to mirror the negative behavior. We reflexively fall into our insecurities and react with our lesser selves. We might lash out or run and hide. Both options waste our time and energy.

Now, imagine how your life would change for the better if you had an "inner peaceful warrior" who gave you the balance and vision to retain your composure, parry your attacker, and take charge of your place in the outcome. Imagine you had an effective system for managing this sort of petty or awkward comment, with graciousness and aplomb. Imagine if you had the skills to reflexively and deftly manage the problem efficiently so that, in the end, not only have you protected yourself, but you have also left the door open for all parties to feel positive about the outcome.

The Soft Answer Verbal T'ai Chi™ is designed to teach you to do exactly this.

The material we have gathered here introduces a practice that has made a significant positive difference in our lives, and we are eager to share it with you. By learning the art of disempowering social and verbal aggression, you are taking steps toward making the world a more peaceful, safer place.

About Us

We (Kat, Monica, Rita, and Susan), are sisters and sisters-in-law with decades of collective experience in education, communication, business, the ins and outs of interpersonal, family, and community dynamics, and T'ai Chi. We discovered, over years of practice, research and discussion, that the self-defense philosophy of T'ai Chi can be applied to social challenges with remarkable results.

Through the cultivation of a Soft Answer practice, we have discovered that it is possible to recognize the imbalance at the core of uncomfortable verbal altercations, and to develop specific skills for restoring balance. As our skills continue to improve, we find that fewer of those imbalanced situations present themselves. It is not that we no longer encounter challenging interactions, but having effective skills gives us confidence that the opportunities for restoring balance often lie in our own hands (and words).

We developed The Soft Answer Verbal T'ai Chi system in order to spread the word about the effective and compassionate communication strategies that have helped bring greater balance and peace into our lives.

A sassafras tree grows in Monica's backyard, where we often met to compile this material. Sassafras trees have four different kinds of leaves: oval, left and right mittens, and three-pronged. We are four very different women with a common family tree, and we made the sassafras tree our symbol. Our company, Sassafras Branches LLC was founded with the mission of helping the world become a kinder, safer place. Monica created the cover image of the four kinds of sassafras leaves using the spectrum of colors the tree displays as it goes through the seasons, with the center image created by putting the four leaves together as one.

Developing the Soft Answer Verbal T'ai Chi system has been a collaborative effort, with all contributions of equal value to the whole. As such, the author listing is in alphabetical order on the cover, but randomized throughout the book.

About T'ai Chi

T'ai Chi Ch'uan (commonly referred to as T'ai Chi) is a system of health and self-defense based on nature's wisdom of balance and harmony. T'ai Chi "players" first learn to move individually. (If you see groups of people moving in unison very slowly on a sunny day in the park, this very well could be T'ai Chi.) Those who study T'ai Chi strive to move with integrity, efficiency, and responsiveness, while staying grounded, centered and balanced. T'ai Chi partner exercises teach people effective skills for responding to and managing incoming energy, and how to avoid getting stuck or hurt when unwelcome energy is coming in.

T'ai Chi philosophy teaches us that it is possible to safely and successfully manage force without contributing undue additional force. Just as nature shows us that one of the most pliable and yielding of substances, water, can also be one of the most powerful, we understand that it is possible to use a soft response to successfully deflect the hardest of incoming forces.

What Verbal T'ai Chi is For

The Soft Answer Verbal T'ai Chi system focuses on how to manage verbal aggression. Uncomfortable verbal interactions can show up almost anywhere: in the workplace, in families, in public...any place two people come into contact and try to communicate. In this book, we teach you to approach challenging verbal interactions using T'ai Chi principles. We stay soft so we can be attentive and appropriately responsive. We relax, and this allows our conversational partners to let go of tension too. We stay open and resilient; we remain centered and whole. We function as part of a system, and act to restore balance.

With Verbal T'ai Chi, you will activate and broaden your existing skills, building on what you already know and what you have already experienced throughout your life. Often, you will do this by taking a fresh look at traditional wisdom.

What Verbal T'ai Chi is Not For

It is critical to be able to recognize when a situation or verbal interaction may be potentially dangerous and responses are necessary which are beyond what we offer in The Soft Answer Verbal T'ai Chi.

For example, the information in this book is *not* for times when:

- someone is threatening physical harm
- there is imminent danger to yourself or others

- an urgent solution is needed to avoid the above.

Any situation like this is beyond the scope of our work. An organization that specializes in these issues can be found in nearly every part of the world. For example, in the United States, you can call the National Coalition Against Domestic Violence hotline.

Find Some Friends

Because we found so much joy and benefit from developing The Soft Answer system collaboratively, we think you will find it enjoyable and useful to explore this material with a friend or small group. Several of our exercises involve working with a partner. Practicing in a group as you develop these skills allows you to bounce ideas off each other and discuss specific problems you might be having.

Another benefit of learning The Soft Answer approach with a friend or group is that you may be able to lift each other's spirits. While verbal aggression can be a sober and challenging subject, learning how to manage it can be a positive experience. By working with friends and people you trust, it can even be a joyful process.

If you can't find a group or partner who wants to develop these skills with you, find a trusted friend and tell this friend about your intention to begin a Soft Answer practice. Ask if he or she would be willing to be a sounding board for you as you go through this material.

Deciding to make a potentially transformational change in your life takes great courage. New ventures can increase vulnerability, opening you to greater risk. Sometimes that may mean letting go of an old habit that, despite the fact that it doesn't serve you well, still feels comforting.

In moments of high emotion, things can temporarily go off the rails, and somewhere along the way you may get frustrated and want to give up. Declaring your intention out loud to a trusted friend means you don't have to go it alone. It gives you a support system.

Structure

Many people like to take in new things slowly, while others want to drink in all they can in one sitting. Some want to proceed systematically, while others prefer a non-linear method. It is important that you feel free to move through this material in a way that best suits the needs of you and your group.

This book can serve as a textbook with many options for structuring your own Soft Answer course. Your group may want to meet monthly, weekly or bi-weekly. Working with one chapter per week will take 24 weeks. Three per week (one for each Monday, Wednesday and Friday for example), gives you an 8 week course. For a week-long workshop, you could cover 4-5 chapters per day; alternatively, you could have an intensive weekend seminar with a review of 8 chapters per day for 3 days (such as covering 3 in the morning, 3 in the afternoon, and 2 in the evening).

Affecting Positive Change

As we continue on our Soft Answer path, we have experienced how, as we affect positive change in ourselves, we are often able to affect positive change in others. It still surprises us how even situations that seem intractable at first can, with soft answers, become amenable to change. People around us often seem more open to cooperative communication.

What if more and more of us developed Soft Answer Verbal T'ai Chi skills? As we continue to take our Soft Answer sensibility out into the world and apply it, we become thought leaders and agents for change every time we demonstrate that Verbal T'ai Chi really works. Others might begin to realize that this option is available to them as well. It is empowering for all of us, and there is great power in groups:

Never doubt that a small group of thoughtful, committed citizens can change the world.[®]*Indeed, it is the only thing that ever has.*

— MARGARET MEAD, USED WITH PERMISSION

We hope that you have fun exploring our Soft Answer philosophy, techniques and exercises, and, if you are doing this with a friend, be sure to bring laughter and joy with you, as these greatly facilitate learning, just as they facilitated the writing of this book.

(Monica, Rita, Susan and Kat)

PART I

GROUNDWORK

1

PURPOSE

The purpose of The Soft Answer Verbal T'ai Chi is to develop internalized skills and resources that provide us with a reflexive kindness and a natural grace in navigating interpersonal exchanges. By respecting and empowering ourselves, we gain the confidence and freedom to respect and empower others. In so doing, we commit to and share in a more balanced, just, and peaceful world.

— Kat, Rita, Monica & Susan

Having a sense of purpose when you set out to do something new can make all the difference. *The Purpose* gives us a framework for the entire Soft Answer Verbal T'ai Chi experience, and a foundation to come back to when we need to regroup.

Let's unpack the *Purpose* statement:

The purpose of The Soft Answer Verbal T'ai Chi is to develop internalized skills and resources...

You will be personalizing useful skills and training yourself to have them at the ready.

...that provide us with a reflexive kindness and a natural grace in navigating interpersonal exchanges...

The power of kindness cannot be overstated. Kindness and grace will be your "go-to" responses, your reflex responses, the responses that emerge without thinking. With enough practice, they can become an intrinsic part of your make-up.

...respecting and empowering ourselves such that we have the confidence and freedom to respect and empower others...

We want to disempower the aggression, but not the person using the misguided tactic of aggression. Authentic power does not need to take away from another; it knows there is no loss in sharing it with others.

Because we feel strong and secure, we can afford to be generous and allow others a graceful way out of a difficult situation. We all deserve to have our dignity and self-respect preserved; that's really the only way to have genuine communication.

...In so doing, we commit to and share in a more balanced, just, and peaceful world.

How will your own expression of *The Soft Answer* manifest itself in the world? How might your life's purpose be advanced by Verbal T'ai Chi?

The Soft Answer is a Practice

Each chapter of this book is a step on your path to a Soft Answer Verbal T'ai Chi practice. We present the principles and related examples, techniques and exercises, but, *you* will be the one making them come alive and customizing them to your own needs by putting them into action. As you do so, you will inevitably meet some bumps in the road along the way. Do not be discouraged.

Remember that millions of people over hundreds of years have found that T'ai Chi Ch'uan really does work. And, verbally, every culture we've come across teaches the wisdom of a Soft Answer philosophy in some way. But, you have to *practice* to get there. Stick with it and you will find that over time, coming up with a soft answer will become more and more natural to you, and success is bound to follow.

Pocket Cards

At the end of each chapter we provide suggestions for reminder cards to carry with you like flash cards. We call them Pocket Cards, and we also furnish a compiled list of all of the Pocket Cards in the Appendix.

Pocket Cards can help you remember specific Soft Answer strategies while you are on the go. You can make them with blank business cards, 3x5 index cards, or whatever else is handy, and in a size that works for you.

Find a handful of Pocket Cards that are especially meaningful for you and carry these with you in a pocket or wallet, or keep them handy in an office or kitchen drawer. Make it part of your routine to take a quick peek at these cards throughout the day so that the ideas can sink in organically and become habit. When you think a verbal altercation may be imminent, you can take a quick look at these to remind yourself of an idea or technique you are learning to apply. Do this often enough, and soon the strategy will come naturally.

For additional ideas on how to make and use Pocket Cards, visit our website: TheSoftAnswer.com and look on the *Resources* page.

Start a Soft Answer Notebook

As you are learning The Soft Answer Verbal T'ai Chi, we suggest you keep a notebook of some kind. You will be creating a record that includes as much detail as you choose. What works? What's confusing? What's hard to remember to do? What feels right (or wrong)?

Your notebook will become a collection of ideas and techniques that work best for you.

Keep your notebook in a place where you can get to it quickly and easily when you have a thought or experience you want to remember. But, we recommend you *not* keep your notebook at work, especially if you are documenting workplace difficulties. If you must make a note when at work, use a documentation method that is private, such as sending a message to yourself on your personal e-mail account. Your Pocket Cards are neutral and are fine to take to work.

Of course, for some of you, a voice or video recording would be a better fit for your particular learning or processing style—that's fine, too. Whatever format you choose, we suggest you create four sections:

General Notes: What makes sense? Is something confusing?

Favorite Strategies: As you go through the book, you can keep a short list of the strategies that work best *for you*. Continually review these strategies as you develop your Soft Answer practice.

Hot Buttons: a list of difficult verbal exchanges or comments that take you by surprise and leave you at a loss for skillful action. (Some of you may choose to put the *Strategies* list and *Hot Buttons* list together, but others may prefer to keep them separate. If you combine these, be sure to stay open to alternative soft answer responses that might be effective to a given verbal incursion.)

Gratitude List: a section reserved for recording anything for which you are grateful. Your gratitude list is a personal reminder of the joys of life. Gratitude allows letting go. It brings humility. Gratitude releases our minds, and draws us into a cycle of joy where expansive solutions, possibilities and opportunities await.

We invite you to write notes directly into this book. This is your workbook and we want you to feel comfortable using it as you need!

2

FIND THE THIRD OPTION

To win without fighting is best.

— Sun Tzu

Anger, fear, aggression - the dark side of the force are they.

— Yoda

We can define aggression as unwelcome incoming force. Common responses to aggressive attitudes include resisting, objecting and avoiding. When you are in a situation in which you are feeling someone else's aggression, these typical "fight or flight" responses (either returning that aggression or recoiling in a fearful way) are ultimately counterproductive. They lead to a win/lose scenario, and most likely lay the groundwork for more confrontational situations in the future.

Look beyond fight or flight and consider a third option. The principle comes from T'ai Chi Ch'uan: *no resistance, no insistence*. It means there is always a skillful response to aggression that avoids both fight and flight and which does not involve unnecessary force. To be able to respond this way, T'ai Chi players need to stay relaxed, and reconfigure their bodies without losing their connection with their partner.

Let's see how this strategy can also be applied in a social situation, with a move we call *Open the Book.*

Open the Book

Open the Book is a simple and effective way to diffuse aggressive behavior. When a person is aggressing, they want to be "in your face" (squarely in front of you). When you learn to *open the book,* you learn how to reposition your body so that your aggressor can not achieve this physical positioning. As you reposition your body, the entire dynamic changes.

Here is how to do it:

Imagine you and your partner (previously known as the "aggressor") are the front and back cover of a book. Decide where the binding/spine of the book would be, and, *open the book.* That is to say, turn your body so that you end up shoulder to shoulder with your partner (but not actually touching), facing the same direction. When the "book" is "closed" (that is, you are face to face), it feels as if the scenario is you against him or her (fight scenario). If you chose to avoid the problem all together (say, by ducking into the nearest hallway or bathroom—flight scenario), this won't solve the problem either. When you *open the book,* it dismisses both the fight and the flight scenario. Instead, it positions you both together, side-by-side against the problem.

An open book is relaxed. It has flexibility. It has possibilities. In *open the book*, we maintain our own central equilibrium, preserving our own well-being and giving our partner the opportunity to preserve themselves as well. This reframes the win/lose scenario so that the outcome has the potential for win/win.

Practicing *open the book* can be quite useful. For this simple, physical exercise you will need a friend. Stand face to face with your friend. Take turns being the person who opens the book and turns to stand shoulder to shoulder with the other person.

When you try to practice this physical technique with someone, you may find yourself in a "freeze" scenario. You stop. You ask yourself, "How do I get my body from this side to that side in an organic way? Which way do I move? How do I turn?" Even in a practice situation, this happens to many people. Go back to the idea of the book. Use this imagery to help your body figure out how to move.

You will want to be able to pull off this movement quickly, subtly and easily. If it feels or looks awkward, you need more practice.

When you are confident with this, try a variation. Have your partner walk toward you and see if you can *open the book* while in motion. As your partner approaches, meet him, *open the book,* and then turn and walk with him, maintaining that open book body language and intention as you walk shoulder to shoulder.

If you feel really comfortable with your partner, take turns trying to "get in their face," and then try opening the book. This extra practice will be helpful if you do encounter a more challenging scenario. Of course, always be respectful and considerate. People have different comfort levels and sensitivities when it comes to physical proximity. At the same time, if you are getting close to the limit of your comfort zone, maybe it is time to take a break.

Even in situations where you cannot manage to get your body to turn all the way to a shoulder to shoulder position with the other person, just see if you can shift slightly in either direction. Even a slightly open book may present an opportunity to allow light and possibility into the interaction.

Practicing *open the book* in a cooperative situation will help you to be able to naturally move into place when someone's aggressive behavior calls for it.

Investing in a Physical Practice

Consider investing in a physical practice, or deepening your commitment to a physical practice you already have.

When you learn something in your body, you learn it in a practical way, and it is different from the kind of learning where you 'get' something intellectually. A physical practice can give you a new kind of confidence and becomes part of your cellular physicality; you can actually improve your instincts and your reflexes by engaging your whole self.

We have seen how practicing T'ai Chi Ch'uan can make this kind of difference. If you can not find a T'ai Chi class in your area, or if T'ai Chi is not to your taste, there are other physical practices and activities you might want to consider, such as fencing, Aikido, Thang Ta or taking an acting or stand up comedy class. Other interactive physical practices and experiences to consider include joining Toastmasters, learning to sing, to sail, to row a boat, taking a class in pottery or welding, or engaging in team sports.

Look for an enjoyable physical practice that heightens your awareness of how you engage in and interact with the world.

Pocket Cards: Open the Book; Find the Third Option

3

COMPASSIONATE DETACHMENT

There is no exercise better for the heart than reaching down and lifting people up.

— JOHN ANDREW HOLMES, JR.

If you want others to be happy, practice compassion. If you want to be happy, practice compassion.

— XIV DALAI LAMA

When someone is not behaving at their best, we want to access and extend a sense of compassion. At the same time, we need to keep enough emotional space so we can feel comfortable and safe. Unless we practice some measure of detachment, we won't have the resources to stay in the game long enough to turn the situation around. *Compassionate Detachment* gives us this crucial balance.

The Soft Answer is a verbal self-defense system that emphasizes the notion that we can let go of our armor without losing our agency. Just as when we *find the third option* we strike a balance between the extremes of fight or flight, in applying *compassionate detachment*, we find the equilibrium between being too distant to make a difference, and being so close that we become helplessly enmeshed. Thinking of it in terms of temperature, we say, *Stay Warm, but Keep your Cool*. This means that we don't want to run too hot or too cold, so we stay warm *externally* (keeping a warm connection to the other person) while we keep our cool *internally* (so we don't get out of balance).

Our ultimate goal is not to suppress a verbal attack, but to *make ourselves immune to the attack*. We do this by listening, staying open, connected, relaxed and empathetic. We start with the assumption that everyone truly wants to be his or her best self at all times. All of this is what allows our compassion to come through.

Cruel or invasive comments may be bait to start an argument, bait to get us to start making excuses, or bait to generate feelings of self-doubt within us. Maybe this person is trying to get under our skin. On the other hand, maybe she is just socially awkward and trying to start a conversation or make a joke. *It doesn't matter.* Our job is to avoid taking the bait (we will go deeper into this in the *Pitfalls* section with chapter 16, *Don't Take the Bait!*). One way to do that is by adjusting our internal response by actively cultivating a state of *compassionate detachment*.

"Poor Thing..."

Suzette Haden Elgin, author of *The Gentle Art of Verbal Self Defense* and related books, identified a couple of very useful statements that exemplify *compassionate detachment*. You don't say these out loud, but you THINK them when someone has made an insensitive comment or has acted without regard to others. The complete statements are:

- *Poor thing. Desperate to communicate and that's the best she (he) can do.*
- *Poor thing. Desperate for attention and that's the best he (she) can do.*

Let's say a guest comes to your house and says, "I love the landscaping that you don't do." The statement itself is what we would call *bait*.

So try this:

Silently say to yourself, "Poor thing. Desperate to communicate and that's the best she can do." Or, "Poor thing. Desperate for attention and this is the best he can do."

Just using these statements of *compassionate detachment* to reframe the entire situation can empower you and can give you the emotional space you need to find a way to respond without taking the bait.

We want to be open to the possibility that, once in a while, something that feels like an attack is actually a heartfelt expression meant to be helpful. The person talking to us is just being awkward. At these times, we want to make an extra effort to be compassionate, and to not be reactive. Compassion is an essential ingredient to our practice.

Remember that there is no need in that moment for us to determine whether this is an actual attack, a gentle ribbing, or a well-meaning, but awkward "helpful criticism." These compassionate yet detached responses will work whatever the case, whereas an anxious counterattack may take someone who is well-meaning into defensive territory and into an attack mode they did not originally intend to be in.

Reflecting with Compassion

Think back to a time when someone made an aggressive comment that left you flustered and speechless. If none comes to mind, take a scene from a movie, book or television show or create one in your imagination. Close your eyes and take a moment to feel yourself in this place. Do you feel relaxed? If not, go back and create some detachment from the situation. Notice where the tension might arise in your body in response to this situation. Breathe into the tension. Try to melt it like warm air on ice. *Compassionate detachment* allows us to remain connected in the recognition that we are all in this together, yet detached in a way that allows us to say, "Your issue does not necessarily have to be my issue."

Now, while you imagine looking at the instigator with sincere compassion, silently say to yourself, "Poor thing. Desperate for attention and that's the best he (or she) can do."

You want to be well-practiced at putting yourself in this mindset, so that when a tirade or inconsiderate flub comes at you in a real-life situation, the thought can bubble up. Then you decide what your next step will be. Accessing this silent statement should guide your next move to be a gracious and compassionate one. Keep your Pocket Cards handy and repeat saying the above phrases over and over to yourself: "Poor thing. Desperate to..."

Remember: You are not trying to turn this person into someone or something pathetic. You are merely recognizing their struggle. At the same time, you are leaving space enough that this person has an opportunity to save face. It might be helpful to think on these phrases if you find yourself faltering: "Create space for saving face" and "Saving face: no disgrace."

Compassion Begins at Home

We will cover this in more depth in Chapter 22, but our experience tells us that our capacity for extending compassion to others is limited only by our capacity to extend compassion to ourselves.

Take care of yourself. Be gentle and compassionate with yourself. Get enough rest and healthy sustenance. Practice forgiveness. If you find yourself in a position where you have just uttered something that is not particularly gracious, you can simply tell yourself, "That was not my best moment; I'll do better next time."

Pocket Cards: Compassionate Detachment; Stay Warm but Keep your Cool; Create Space for Saving Face; Saving Face: No Disgrace; Think: "Poor thing. Desperate to communicate and that's the best she (or he) can do"; Think: "Poor thing. Desperate for attention and that's the best he (or she) can do"

PART II

AWARENESS

4

PAY ATTENTION

The most important thing in communication is hearing what isn't said.

— PETER DRUCKER

When you really pay attention, everything is your teacher.

— EZRA BAYDA

Awareness is fundamental to understanding what is happening, both around us and within us. The more we understand, the more skillfully we can act and react when someone lashes out.

We aim to cultivate our ability to *pay attention*, both to ourselves and to others, and then add the skill of being able to *Listen Deeply*, both internally and externally, in a relaxed way, without preconceived notions or rushing to judgment.

We can deliberately improve our ability to *pay attention* by observing people more closely. This is something we can do everywhere, whenever we think of it. Notice people's body language. Notice whether they carry themselves in a tense, closed position or whether they are more open and relaxed. What is happening with a given person's facial muscles and hand gestures? Notice tone of voice and choice of words that are used. Who is looking to communicate with others, and who seems to want to confront others?

We want to listen without internalizing any negative emotions that we might observe. It is also important to remember to attend *without being judgmental.* Being judgmental puts us in a closed position and will inhibit our listening ability. Merely notice what people are conveying.

Allow paying attention to others to become a habit. It is amazing what we can learn just from this.

Consider writing down some of your observations and thoughts in your Soft Answer notebook. If you are having a hard time figuring out what specific body positions might mean, consider exploring online resources on body language or pick up a book on body language at the library.

Listen Deeply

Listening might take some getting used to. It may feel as if you are not actually doing anything. Ah, but you are not "just listening"! Listening deeply and openly, with curiosity and an investigative framework, is a completely engaged experience. It is active, not passive. It is intentional, not involuntary. When we *pay attention* and *listen deeply,* it can take the surprise element out of many verbal volleys; we are more inclined to notice an attack coming, and may find we have the time to respond in a more skillful and effective way.

"Tell Me More"

When we *listen deeply* and *pay attention,* it is as if we are nonverbally inviting anyone and everyone, "Tell me more." As it turns out, actually asking someone to "Tell me more," can be a very useful technique, especially when someone is agitated, aggressive or complaining.

Generally, when a person is sending a verbal charge in your direction, the last thing they expect is for you to ask for more information. The element of surprise can be very powerful, and that alone might lead someone to reconsider his approach. Additionally, aggressors are generally prepared for a fight, not straightforward cooperation or gentle curiosity. Your lack of defensiveness or counter-attack compels them to reconfigure.

Be forewarned: this will only work if you are completely sincere and emotionally neutral and centered. Do not derail yourself by indulging in negativity or going in with a cynical attitude that you are tricking the other person. That will have the opposite effect from what you are intending.

There are a number of phrase variations you can try. Find one that fits your personality and situation. Here are some examples:

- *Tell me more, if you don't mind.*
- *Hmmm...that didn't occur to me...can you tell me more about that?*
- *Huh! I never would have thought about it that way. Please, go on.*
- *That's such an interesting perspective; can you talk a bit more about that?*
- *Would you mind expanding on the idea of ...? I'd really appreciate it.*

Asking for more information from your conversational partner allows you an opportunity to listen more deeply to the other person. When you listen with an open heart, without preconceptions or without expectations of conflict, you again position yourself to be joining the other person in problem solving rather than positioning yourself for battle. This is a way of connecting and letting them know they are not alone.

Practicing with Verbal Attacks

Movies and TV can be great sources of verbal attacks to practice with. For example, watch the comedy-drama *The Women* (either the 1939 version or the 2008 remake). Find a scene with a verbal attack that interests you.

Play the scene you have selected and *listen deeply* to the sequence of events. How does it start? How does it develop? How does it end?

Then, listen and watch again, but this time, imagine yourself in the role of the attacker. What would cause someone to behave this way? Put yourself in her place. What kind of body language is she using? What kind of tone? Can you imagine yourself saying this to someone, ever? How would it feel?

Play the scene a third time and put yourself in the position of the one being attacked. What does the body language look like here? What is the attitude and tone of voice? How is this person responding to the attack? Why? Is the response a skillful one? Is it working out well? What causes someone to respond this way? Can you think of a more productive response that would bring a more positive outcome? What would have happened, do you think, if the target of the aggression responded by asking for more information: "Tell me more…"?

Of course this is not real-life, but it is a comfortable, non-threatening, easy way to start practicing listening deeply while you are participating in a challenging interaction. Theater is often based, at least partially, on the real life experiences of the playwright.

After this, you will be more ready to include a measure of detachment when you observe a verbal struggle, or when you get caught up in one, especially after you ask someone to tell you more. At any time, listening deeply is a very useful habit, but it takes practice.

All this information can be added to your research notes, and later you can use it to create, test and develop new techniques to help you on your journey with *The Soft Answer*.

Pocket Cards: "Tell Me More"; Pay Attention; Listen Deeply

5

RELAX AND LISTEN INTERNALLY

If you know the enemy and know yourself, you need not fear the result of a hundred battles.

— Sun Tzu

The wise one breathes to the bottom of the heels.

— Chuang Tzu

We have looked at the importance of being able to *pay attention* and *listen deeply* to others so we can better learn what is going on when someone is behaving in a verbally combative way. But, as Sun Tzu points out in the quote from the *Art of War* that appears above, knowing the "enemy" is not enough. If we want to be able to face hostility fearlessly, we must also know ourselves. In The Soft Answer program we do not regard the other person as an enemy per se, but nonetheless, we agree with Sun Tzu that learning about our opponent is only useful if we are also actively learning about ourselves.

This is why we train ourselves to become better listeners of our own internal environments, consciously deepening our ability to *Relax and Listen Internally*. It gives our stress management skills a boost, and increases our effectiveness in using soft answers.

Cultivating Relaxation

The central principle that makes T'ai Chi Ch'uan successful as a system of self-protection, health and meditation is *relaxation*. We are taught that these three aspects (self-protection, health and meditation) may be regarded as the legs of a three-legged stool: all three have to be in place for T'ai Chi to work. All three start with relaxation and succeed because of relaxation.

Relaxation and Self Protection: Now that you are paying closer attention to verbal squabbles, have you noticed that, no matter what happens, the most relaxed person is the one who really "wins"? Even if that person loses materially, the psychic loss is on the side of the one who gets pulled into the system of fighting on an emotional level.

In an altercation, *tension provides a handle for an adversary to gain advantage.* Relaxation denies him or her this handle, while simultaneously allowing us to listen and perceive where our adversary's tension is, which in turn gives us a strategic advantage. We cannot respond skillfully to verbal aggression if we cannot *relax*, because we won't be able to think clearly. It is relaxation that allows us to pay close attention, and it is relaxation that is essential to our success. Our relaxation is our protection.

When we can stay relaxed in the face of interpersonal tension, we typically discover that we have more options. We can respond skillfully by staying connected with the other person. We are able to observe the tension until we find an opportunity to redirect it with just the slightest effort, and so diffuse (and de-fuse) the force of the attack.

Just like the T'ai Chi master who catches the cup before she even realizes it is falling, relaxed soft answers and effective actions can become automatic responses that effortlessly emerge from us at just the right moment. But, in order for this to happen spontaneously, we have to practice—a lot.

Relaxation and Health: Verbal attacks are stressors. Stress run amok can leave us physically, mentally and psychologically compromised, not just in the moment that the stress event is happening, but in the hours, days, and even years after (for example with PTSD).

The physical damage of stress can even extend down to the subcellular level, as recent studies have shown: even our telomeres, which provide a protective casing to our DNA strands, can become damaged by stress, and the more stress we're managing, the more our body's ability to repair the telomeres can be compromised. The damage that results is associated with accelerated aging, as the cell may die or even become pro-inflammatory (APA.org Vol 45, No. 9, 2014).

Relaxation, on the other hand, can help keep us healthy. It helps protect the heart, lowers risk of everything from stroke to catching a cold, and can improve our memory, our ability to manage recovery from illness, and our ability to make better decisions (Huffington-Post.com, 8/14/2014).

Relaxation and Meditation: There are many ways to meditate. Common to almost all is cultivating awareness and being awake to the present moment. In T'ai Chi, relaxation allows us to increase awareness, because we can *pay attention* better when we are free of excess anxiety. That includes paying attention to the inner workings and flow of our own bodies. The T'ai Chi classics advise us to keep our bodies stable and comfortable.

Listen Internally

Our bodies, including our breathing, reflect our emotional states. Often when we get nervous or anxious (for example, when someone is assailing us socially), we inhale and may even hold our breath. When we hold our breath and tense up, we are in a fear response. Fortunately, things can work both ways, and we can deliberately work with our breathing to calm the body and our emotional state. But, we can only do this if we are paying attention and are aware of what's going on with us internally.

This one can be hard to do in a difficult moment, because our conversational partner's stress can pull our attention like a magnet. To get ourselves into the habit of listening internally, we have to practice when there is no agitation in the air.

If you stand, sit or lie down comfortably in a quiet place, you can begin to tune in to your internal climate.

An easy place to start is with rhythms. Tune in to the pace, depth and rhythm of your breathing. What else can you notice? Can you feel your pulse or your heartbeat? Acupuncturists train themselves to feel six different meridian pulses in each wrist, and some people can feel their own craniosacral rhythms. It's amazing how we can improve our ability to "hear" what's happening in our internal environment if we continue to quietly *pay attention*.

Breathing and Meditation

Meditation and breathing are intimately connected. An easy way to start meditating is with a conscious exhale. Focus on your exhale as you breathe. Many meditation systems recommend making the exhale longer than the inhale, and breathing in and out through the nose. Try this, making sure you are exhaling fully. Notice the effect this has on your whole body.

To continue your exploration of breathing and meditation, go through the material below as slowly and as many times as you like. The key is to be mindful and feel comfortable. If you will be standing, be sure not to lock your knees. If you will be sitting, be sure not to slump. Lying down? ...well, just try not to fall asleep.

Meditation Exercise: Find a comfortable position. If sitting or standing, see if, by adjusting the tilt of your hips, you can find a "sweet spot" where your spine can feel effortlessly open, so you can be relaxed. When your spine is like this, your torso is free to move, so it's easier to breathe.

Again, take a breath. Notice where your inhale goes. Exhale. What changes?

Take another breath. While you breathe in, send your mind to your neck. As you exhale, let the muscles in your neck release any tension.

On your next inhale, send your mind to your shoulders, elbows and wrists, and on the exhale allow them to release.

On the following inhale, send your mind to the lower part of your lungs. Can you draw your inhale deeply, such that your breath reaches the lower part of your lungs? Again, exhale and *Relax*.

On your next inhale, see if you can feel your abdomen expand. Exhale.

With another breath—can you bring your mind to your hip joints, knees and ankles? Exhale and let go of any tension you feel there.

Now notice: Has your breath changed? Try to breathe slowly and quietly. Breathe to the bottom of your feet.

When you are ready to end your meditation, allow yourself to come out of it slowly and gently.

Relax. Rinse. Repeat (as necessary).

THE NEXT TIME YOU ARE IN A SITUATION WHERE THE CONVERSATIONAL temperature is starting to rise, try to *Relax*, breathe and remember your meditative state. Although, easier said than done, you will be developing a strategy of relaxing under pressure.

Regulating your breathing helps to re-set your systems and can buy valuable time in a difficult conversation. It can slow things down enough that you may be able to avoid being pulled into someone else's state of anxiety. Breathe quietly while you are doing your deep listening. This politely applies the brakes on unnecessary urgency and can put the other person's agenda into perspective.

We emphasize breathing *quietly,* especially while you are exhaling. You don't want to sound as if you are sighing. Sighs can be perceived as aggressive and may just make your conversational partner more agitated.

Suppose someone approaches you and wants you to think that his or her issue is the most urgent and immediately important thing in the world. Remember, anything that comes out of your mouth when you're in a state of agitation is likely to get you into trouble. Instead, the best advice we can give you is, when things get tough, remember to ...

Breathe...

Sometimes you need a moment so you can figure out how to respond without adding fuel to the fire.

Breathe...

Silently, softly, and with an attitude of attentiveness to the person coming at you,

Breathe...

Stay focused. You are considering carefully; you want to avoid overreacting. You also want the other person to know that you do care about what he or she has to say.

Breathe...

Other Relaxation Strategies

In *Find the Third Option*, we suggested that you start a physical practice. Some, such as T'ai Chi, Aikido, yoga, Qi Gong or I Ch'uan can also serve as meditative practices. Or, how about taking a class in meditation?

Not a "joiner"? Swimming, running, walking, gardening, cooking, knitting...almost any solo physical activity can become a meditative practice, increasing awareness. There are lots of clips on YouTube and other such sites with online classes, and there are podcasts and apps for your digital devices out there as well.

We also recommend reading or listening to books about meditation, such as:

- *The Relaxation Response* by Herbert Benson

- *A Path With Heart* by Jack Kornfield
- *Progressive Relaxation* by Edmund Jacobson
- *Taking the Path of Zen* by Robert Aitken
- *Full Catastrophe Living* by Jon Kabat-Zinn

Don't like to read? Spend more time in silence. Sit in front of a warm fire. Take a bath. Spend more time in nature (outside, at the zoo, in the park, by the water). Try a biofeedback device or game. Hum. Yawn and stretch.

Get creative: paint, draw, model with clay, play a harmonica, dance...the experience of relaxation and increased internal awareness is what is important, not the product.

Pocket Cards: Relax; Breathe; Listen to Your Body; Listen Internally; Pay Attention to Your Breath; Cultivate Relaxation; Our relaxation is our protection

6

START FRESH, STAY OPEN

I keep my ideals, because in spite of everything I still believe that people are really good at heart.

— ANNE FRANK

A mind is like a parachute. It doesn't work if it is not open.

— FRANK ZAPPA

Start Fresh reminds us to deal with others without pre-judging them or making assumptions. *Stay Open* reminds us to maintain a non-judgmental position, and to stay "in the moment" in the face of aggression. We let go of negative feelings and we let go of expectations. Negative attitudes keep us stuck in the past. Expecting a specific outcome keeps us attached to an unknowable future. Both pull us away from present moment awareness.

Learning how to *start fresh* and *stay open* takes practice, so in this chapter we are giving you a few different ways to work with the concept.

"Interesting…"

We have discussed how to *find the third option*, and the importance of being compassionate and attentive. The technique of responding with a non-committal, open ended comment such as, "Interesting…," is a way to indicate that we are keeping an open mind, and this integrates well with other Soft Answer strategies.

The key is to respond attentively while not being the slightest bit sarcastic or critical. Both sarcasm and criticism are evidence that a judgment has been made. As soon as we become judgmental, our perspective begins to narrow. This can be a slippery slope to closed-mindedness. If the person whose pugnacity we need to deal with is close to us and there is a history of serial aggression, letting this person know that we are interested and we are listening can help both of us avoid getting stuck in a familiar trap of pushing buttons and allowing buttons to be pushed.

Here are a few variations on this theme:

- *I never would have thought of that.*
- *That's a surprising question (point, perspective, angle on this, consideration).*
- *I'll have to think about it.*
- *Hmmmm…I wonder…*
- *Really? Well that's something…*
- *What an interesting (unexpected, original, curious) thought.*

If someone is complaining or accusing:

- *It can be so frustrating when you feel you're not being understood (listened to, respected, …).*

It is important to realize that listening carefully for instances in which the other person is right or wrong is *not* suspending judgment; it is the opposite. Justification leads us into the trap of angling and planning witty retorts. While these may yield temporary satisfaction, they are ultimately fear-based actions, and are not part of a Soft Answer practice.

Rewiring Negative Patterns

We can help others rewire their negative patterns by using the technique of *Flipping Negativity*. Some people always seem to say "no," no matter what the occasion. If we are working with someone like this, we may be able to short-circuit their habitually oppositional pattern by inverting the way we might normally ask a question. For example, instead of saying, "Would you like to go to the store with me?", we can say, "You wouldn't want to go to the store with me, would you?"

If they say, "No,'" as you anticipated, they may be surprised to find themselves agreeing to go to the store with you. If they say, "You're right. I don't want to go," at least you have gotten them to agree with you on something!

For people who often exhibit opposition, they may be reflexively disagreeing without really considering the question. They may not even want to say no, but they may be trapped in their own habitual negative patterns. So, to turn a habitual negative response around, we phrase the lead in question in a way that potentially elicits agreement.

Flip negativity by using the frame: "You wouldn't want to..., would you?" Both components are important. First you presume the negative by saying, "you wouldn't want to...," and then you put the ball in their court by asking "would you?"

Improvise!

In his 2007 book, *Blink*, Malcolm Gladwell writes about improvisational comedy. There is a governing principle that in order to succeed, you have to "agree" with whatever comes at you. No matter how outrageous the statement another person on stage throws at you,

you never object. Instead, you behave as if it is a completely reasonable statement and go on from there. Improvisation requires starting fresh and staying open.

You can apply this method of agreement in Verbal T'ai Chi. Keep an open mind and find a way to stay in the conversation. Starting fresh and staying open keeps you connected, but agenda-free, just as in finding a third option.

If this seems wrongheaded (why would we want to appear to agree with someone who is totally off-base?), remember that disagreeing puts us in a "fight" position, and our goal is to avoid buying in to that framework. Secondly, disagreeing does nothing to motivate the other person to reconsider their perspective, and may accomplish just the opposite: they dig their heels right in.

Consider this: *being agreeable* is different from agreeing. It takes a fresh, non-judgmental position and conveys, "I acknowledge that this is your current view on the subject." This puts us in a critically different position. We are not opposite. We are psycho-emotionally shoulder to shoulder.

To get an idea about how to do this, try doing a simple improvisational theater exercise with someone. One person says outrageous, far-fetched and provocative things. The other person figures out how to stay connected, listening and open, until he can find something to agree with.

Improvisation exercises can be fun and hilarious, but when there is a real-life verbal provocation at hand, we do not want to try to be funny. We have to be completely sincere in order for this to work. But improvising with a friend is training, so it's okay to be funny—the exercise should be fun. Training develops our neutral improvisational skill set. The skill of improvisation and being able to respond without being thrown is a key piece to how The Soft Answer system works. We get better by practicing, and, in order to make these skills (staying neutrally non-judgmental and improvising) easier, we can even be funny if we want. In a real instance of verbal aggression it's probably best to avoid humor: save it for practice with friends!

A: You just don't understand.

B: You're very possibly right on that point.

A: You think you know everything.

B: I guess I'll have to think about that.

You get the idea. If you have been keeping a Soft Answer notebook and have a *Hot Buttons* list of verbal annoyances and such, you might try pulling them out now.

If you discover a response that works particularly well for you, make yourself a Pocket Card.

Stick Lightly

Recall that to *find the third option* means avoiding both fight and flight. It requires staying with the opponent in a neutral way without resorting to these two extremes. Try this physical exercise which helps you develop an attentive, responsive, non-judgmental, neutral and open mind:

Standing next to and a little behind your partner, put your hand with open palm lightly at the top corner of your partner's back, near the shoulder. The goal is to have a very soft connection, such that your partner can feel the presence of your hand, but not the *weight* of your hand. Ask your partner to move around the room slowly enough so that you can stick lightly. As you follow, keep this light, soft connection as consistent as possible.

Ideally your partner/leader moves about within your comfortable range of motion—there is no need to make this highly challenging, although it's fine to be playful. Keep it pretty easy so both of you can stay relaxed. Then, switch roles. As you and your partner get better at this, you can start to make the movements a little more random, which will increase the challenge.

Just as in a conversation, we do not know which way our partner is going to move next. This exercise helps us understand that we don't *need* to know, either. We just need to stay attentive, and lightly connected, to stick and to follow.

Especially with difficult conversations, this skill is invaluable.

Pocket Cards: Start Fresh, Stay Open; Don't Rush to Judgment; Keep an Open Mind; "Interesting…"; Stick Lightly

PART III

ATTITUDES

7

JOY IS THE SKILL OF SKILLS

Do what brings you joy, and your purpose will unfold.

— Iyanla Vanzant

Be sincere; be brief; be seated.

— Franklin D. Roosevelt (by way of James Roosevelt, recalling his father's advice on the essence of public speaking)

I f you need to address an issue that has the potential to be a point of contention, how can you take the weight of emotionality out of the dialogue? If you suspect you are under attack, it can be beneficial to use as few words as possible to get your point across.

Levity and Brevity

Using *Levity and Brevity* creates an opportunity for us to let something go more easily. Strategically, this can help to keep us from becoming enmeshed emotionally when someone tries to "bait" us, or pull us into their emotional reality system.

What helps us keep it light and brief? We come from a place of joy.

Suzette Haden Elgin, in *The Gentle Art of Verbal Self-Defense*, wrote, "Joy is the skill of skills." Being joyful is one of the simplest responses to a verbal attack. It turns out that it also can keep you from being a verbal attacker!

Imagine a spectrum with love and joyfulness on one end, and fear and resentment on the other. Picking a fight with a joyful person is a very difficult thing to do. Imagine the most joyful person you know. Where could you even begin if you wanted to pick a fight with him or her? Being joyful means that an aggressor can be completely disarmed before she even begins.

Instigators need to connect before they can incite. If an aggressor approaches a person who is joyful, unabashedly cheerful, light-hearted and bright eyed, he will know, somewhere inside, that he will have to soften up a bit in order to connect. He will sense how the extreme mismatch will not work.

To flow through life's difficult moments, we can cultivate what the French call *joie de vivre* (the joy of living). We are not talking about being funny or clownish and we don't have to be giddy to be joyful. Joy comes from a sense of inner peace. It is centered. It is grounded. It blooms. Joy can be subtle and quiet. It does not have to be loud.

Smile

Research tells us that smiling is good for us physically, neurochemically and psychologically. There are even meditation teachings that have you smile inwardly to your organs. A simple smile can be a powerful thing.

1) Sit or lie down comfortably in a quiet place and simply smile. Breathe and smile, Relax any tension in your facial muscles and

notice how you are feeling. Notice how smiling influences your feeling.

2) Today, as you walk around, notice who is smiling and who is not. Decide to be one of the smiling people. Smile at others who smile. And, smile at those who do not. It can be a small quiet smile. Your smile should match your style and be sincere. You are extending compassion and spreading optimism and joy.

3) Try this in a one-on-one situation when you get a chance, preferably under circumstances that are only slightly challenging. You can try the more difficult people later. Be joyful. Smile (with connection and compassion—don't be overbearing).

See what happens.

Revisit Gratitude to Access Joy

Taking an "attitude of gratitude" is a skill that can be cultivated. Take a look at the *Gratitude List* section in your Soft Answer notebook where you write things for which you are grateful. (If you have none, then take a moment to think of a few.) As we said in our introduction, gratitude allows us to let go. It brings us humility. And it reminds us of the things for which we should be joyful.

Suggested Reading

In meditation, we need to be willing to let go of everything in our mind except the object of the meditation. We need to be willing to be empty. In his book, *After the Ecstasy, the Laundry,* by Jack Kornfield tells of Ajahn Jumnien, a Malaysian monk who came to the U.S. to teach. The monk in this story knew almost no English, but he was able to teach a full lesson by repeating the phrase, "Empty, empty—happy, happy."

Creative Visualization, by Shakti Gawain, is a treasure of a book that gives us many practical ways to discover the joyfulness that is already in our lives.

In Chapter 50 of the *Tao Te Ching*, a person is described who lives so far from fear that she needs no armor when she goes into battle, a person who is not endangered by spear, nor tiger's claw nor rhinoceros' horn. This person is so full of life that such things cannot find a place to enter. When we come from a place of joy, it is as if there is nothing that can bother us—pugnacity cannot catch an edge; belligerence finds no ground.

When two Nobel laureates become fast friends and collaborate on a book about the importance of joy, you know it is time to pay attention. The Rev. Desmond Tutu's visit to the Dalai Lama for his 80th birthday celebration resulted in *The Book of Joy: Lasting Happiness in a Changing World* (co-authored with Doug Abrams).

Pocket Cards: Be Joyful; Smile; Levity and Brevity; Whatever You Feed Will Grow

8

BE SINCERE

Sincerity is impossible, unless it pervade the whole being, and the pretense of it saps the very foundation of character.

— JAMES RUSSELL LOWELL

Truth is such a rare thing, it is delightful to tell it.

— EMILY DICKINSON

When we are managing verbal aggression, it is essential to *Be Sincere*. Sincerity has a quality similar to being joyful. It makes it very difficult for a would-be instigator to "catch an edge" and succeed in starting an argument.

If your conversational companion is trying to pull you into an emotional tangle, saying something honest and being sincere can help you stay grounded and not get wound up.

Being sincere can be helpful for responding to an uncomfortable verbal surprise, because it keeps you in the conversation. But, your statement must be said sincerely and in a neutral tone. It is also fine to add a sprinkle of brightness and friendliness if appropriate to the situation. Levity and brevity!

It's helpful to practice saying your honest responses in advance, either to yourself or with a friend or small group. Even if it is unlikely that they will apply perfectly in a future verbal tussle, practicing will orient you to giving this kind of reply. Write down any lines that seem to work particularly well for you in the *Favorite Strategies* section of your Soft Answer notebook.

Say Something True

Quarrels often have emotional components which go beyond issues of correcting misinformation or making sure the other person is accurate.

If quarrels were solely about provable accuracy, these situations could be easily resolved, and would not become as fervent as they do. Verbal squabbles are almost always about the heightened psycho-emotional states of those involved. Speaking truthfully can be one way to stay in the game without adding fuel to that fire.

We can practice the useful tactic *Say Something True* by finding something to say that cannot really be argued with, either because it is generally accepted as true, or because it's true personally, either for the other person or for us.

It's generally accepted as true: Let's first consider statements which might generally be accepted as true. This kind of truth is usually going to be perceived as neutral material. Facts fall into this category, as do comments that may be considered obvious. In a normal, friendly conversation, you probably don't want to waste time stating the obvious, but when someone is levying a verbal assault, it can be a useful tool.

∾

CONSIDER THESE STATEMENTS:

- *That was a pretty crowded event.*
- *Lots of people lose their jobs unexpectedly.*
- *This is quite a party.*
- *There may be a lot of people who feel that way.*
- *I suppose they have their reasons.*
- *Losing things can be very frustrating.*

Again, your goal is to stay in the conversation, but not take part in furthering any aggressive, devious or bullying agenda.

It's true for you: You can use personal truths when you say something true, making a neutral, personally true statement. Saying something that is true for you is to flatly deliver a personal truth that cannot really be argued with, because it is your personal truth (although be careful: it can be belittled or written off—just another form of verbal attack).

- *I just didn't care for that movie.*
- *I always like seeing people enjoying themselves.*
- *It feels like there's something here that I don't understand.*
- *It's hard for me to know right now what will happen next Thursday.*

You can also use this technique when someone makes an inappropriate personal comment, such as, "You're not wearing THAT, are you?" A few ideas:

- *I feel so good when I wear this.*
- *Aunt Rose gave this to me; I wanted her to see how much I'm enjoying it.*

...or you can simply say, *I am.*

It's true for *them*: Imagine someone says something outrageous. Because you are looking for ways to defuse this particular bomb, *listen deeply* to what the *other person* presents as true. Another person's truth can be informative and helpful to your success in dissipating a conflict. And, whether or not you also think it is true is immaterial to your goal of trying to get through the conversation gracefully.

We attend to whatever the other person thinks is true because it is the truth that belongs to that person, no matter how dubious it may sound to us at that moment. Just as someone else can not really argue with what is true for you, it is helpful to accept that what someone else says is true for them is a kind of truth as well, whether you agree with it or not.

If something is true for someone else, there is not much value in trying to argue against it. There is little chance that you will change their mind, and the most likely outcome will be that they harden their position.

The question to ask yourself is, "How can I connect with this perspective and still be honest and sincere?" Here are some ideas:

- *Well, you've certainly given me something to think about.*
- *It sounds like you've thought about this a lot.*
- *I hear what you're saying, I'm just not quite sure what it means.*
- *I have no doubt there are others who would agree with you.*
- *It's an interesting perspective you have; I'm not sure I share it, though.*
- *Wow, I guess I never looked at it that way...*

If you are listening carefully, you may be able to find agreement with a truth inside someone else's truth. Consider this conversation:

A: I did months of hard work to make this thing come off without a hitch. You didn't even thank me!
B: I know you put a huge amount of time and effort into this project (event/meeting/party). Thank you.

Notice that you are not saying that their efforts succeeded or were even useful to the process. This person may even have been an obstacle. Your move is to sincerely acknowledge that they made an effort.

You might want to try these techniques with some of the verbal jabs you have been recording in the *Hot Buttons* section of your Soft Answer notebook. Just remember to remain sincere, truthful, respectful and kind.

What the other person thinks of as true is of interest to you because it is useful. You're not concerned with evaluating its veracity, and you are not going to convince someone that something is not true if she thinks it is true. Simply attend to whatever the other person thinks is true. If you are dealing with this person, you will be dealing with her truths. It's helpful to be informed.

Being a Bit Less Than True

Lastly, keep in mind the words of John Lily, who said, "What you believe to be true is true, within certain limits, which are themselves beliefs." So, when it comes to determining what is true, it might be useful to practice a bit of flexibility.

In some cases, it may be ethically acceptable to say something that is less than true.

In Amsterdam during the WWII German occupation, when asked "Is the Frank family here? Have you seen them?" an act of integrity would be to lie—even if they were upstairs hiding in your attic.

"I can't right now, I have a hair appointment"—might not be true, but sometimes it might be the kinder thing to say.

Some people can argue with any statement, it seems, but the point here is that if you say something that is true for you, or something that is fairly obvious or agreed upon as "true," the statement may allow you to stay connected to your conversational partner without fueling the fire, and puts the ball in their court for the next move.

Can you say your piece with honesty and sincerity, and then just calmly wait? Can you be patient and generous and give the other person plenty of time and space to respond? You cannot control other people, but you can control yourself. No technique is guaranteed to work all the time, and if you have tried a few things and your conversational partner is still bellicose, try being joyful or compassionate. And, if that doesn't work, remember that you can always politely excuse yourself.

Pocket Cards: Say Something True; Be Sincere

9

LOW DRAMA

Whatever you feed will grow.

— Suzette Haden Elgin

Negative people need drama like oxygen. Stay positive, it will take their breath away.

— MJ Korvan and Tony Gaskins (attributed to both)

High drama situations are hazardous. Avoid getting wound up and sucked in. *Low Drama* means staying emotionally neutral, not adding fuel to the fire.

Low drama also means that your responses should be like water: immediately responsive, seeking a pathway of least resistance, and flowing to the lowest level. When a small pebble drops into a still pool, the response is instantaneous. It is also proportionally appropriate to the event: water always behaves in measure. When the pebble has fallen beneath the surface of a pool, the surface smooths out again and returns to stillness; it does not hold onto the agitation.

In seeking that path of least resistance, water flows around whatever it meets; it does not resist or insist. By its nature it flows with and around responsively. This is why, in martial arts, we cultivate having a "mind like water." Think of it this way: anytime we overreact to the actions of another, we have given that person control over us, and we no longer have a mind like water.

Being *low drama* also means staying centered, rather than heading out to the extremes. Think about how we use the phrase "losing it." What are we losing? We are losing our feeling of being centered, and also our temper, our "cool." Any extreme is a problem. Whether our reaction to aggression is to get heated up (getting hot under the collar) or to freeze (turning a cold shoulder and freezing the other person out), both ways we end up losing out. So, the Soft Answer's *low drama* approach is to try to keep ourselves on the middle ground. As we discussed in *compassionate detachment*, we keep our cool while maintaining a warm attitude towards others: *Stay Warm but Keep your Cool.*

Sometimes people seek to pull conversations into a high drama mode to scratch an itch they have; a high drama state can stimulate them in a way that helps them manage their own restlessness. Whether they have innocent or negative motives, our response is the same. We want to transmit the message that they can try to provoke us, but it is not going to be effective. We stay connected, which means we stay present and responsive to the moment, but we also apply *compassionate detachment* to keep ourselves feeling comfortable and safe.

Leveling

Leveling involves being direct, honest and frank: "on the level." Leveling can mean being calm and steady or taking action that smooths out the highs and lows and makes things flatter. We can keep our voice level, and we can take action that "levels the playing field." In the technique of leveling, we use the term in all of these senses.

When someone is misbehaving verbally, we are not going to get riled up. We're going to be straight with this person. When the situation calls for it, we politely cut through the niceties and are direct: we level with them. But, to make this work, we must be absolutely sincere. We must be confident, conveying with our body, vocal tone, eyes, everything: "It really doesn't matter what you throw at me. I'm confident that I can manage it."

Some examples of leveling might be:

- *That was not a very kind thing to say.*
- *I hear what you're saying, but I don't see that happening.*
- *Why, exactly, are you saying this to me?*

Leveling and maintaining a *low drama* position is a delicate art, but, deftly applied, it can keep you connected with a rabble-rouser without satisfying his need to escalate things emotionally.

How Low Can You Go?

How *low drama* can you go? In some circumstances, you might want to try the strategy of deliberately being a little boring. We have found that it's possible to *Take your Time*, go for a *Low Drama* state, and even be a little dull and tedious, but still *be sincere* and maintain integrity.

To clarify, it is not that you would want to be dull or tedious under normal conditions. But when someone is behaving badly, and very possibly deliberately so, it would be silly to deny this reality and respond as if everything *were* normal. You are no longer in the realm of ordinary, friendly conversation, so, even though you still want to *be sincere* and polite, your colleague's actions have taken the conversation outside the bounds of polite social behavior. You need a response that works with what is being delivered, yet you can still be perfectly civilized, sincere, and kind.

Let's say someone suddenly and wrongly accuses you: "Why did you cut in front of me in the line?" You could be caught off guard.

Being boring is a way to create a trough to divert and absorb the excess emotional wave of the aggressor.

Particularly when the scenario inside the head of the person coming at you with a verbal charge doesn't seem to be based in any shared reality, being boring, flat and neutral is not unkind. It can even be seen as a kindness, because you are not contributing to the reality distortion field this person is in. You are disempowering the aggressive behavior without disempowering the person.

While you have no obligation to play a game someone is trying to force you into, *you do have an obligation to maintain your own agency and integrity.*

We are not talking about being provocative. The strategy of being boring should not be used with the intent of provoking someone. Let's say someone is trying to get personal information from you and is being disruptive and interruptive. They are importuning. You do not want to provoke this person and you also don't want to give them information for which they have no right to be asking.

Perhaps you have the confidence to say, "I don't believe I'm obliged to share that information with you." or, "My personal information is just exactly that: personal." And then leave. But, if you don't have that level of confidence and skill yet, you need another tactic, and maybe, for some of you, being boring (while still being kind and respectful) is an easier way to deliver a Soft Answer.

EXAMPLES OF TEDIOUS RESPONSES:

A: "Give me your name. I want to know your name so I can tell everyone what you've done here."

B: "I completely understand why someone might be motivated to ask another person for their name, and I am quite sure that there are a number of people who would feel very comfortable giving their name out to perfect strangers, and maybe even their addresses...or perhaps they would agree to show an ID, like their driver's license or their passport, if they even carry one with them, because not everyone does, of course, but..."

A: "You're not really GOING to that, are you?"

B: "The processes people go through and the considerations they make when they are trying to determine whether or not to attend various functions or participate in certain events on particular occasions can be completely mysterious, ..."

Applied with confidence, sincerity and respect, being boring can be a very helpful strategy.

Practicing Leveling and Low Drama

• Observe when the drama level of a situation increases and intensifies. This is easier to do when you are an observer and not one of the main players in the tussle.

• Notice how it feels to maintain a relaxed, comfortable, low drama, and level state. Practice invoking this state when things start winding up around you, and keep practicing.

• Learn about the Danish traditional low drama practice of hygge. There are lots of books, articles and websites about how to cultivate this gentle and low drama lifestyle that celebrates comfort, ease, and coziness.

• Ask a friend to deliver some of the verbal bombs you have in the *Hot Buttons* section of your notebook. Take your time in responding and try to stay low drama and level. If you do not have a friend to help you, try this: make an audio recording of a verbal attack, then play the recording back to hear the aggressive words coming at you. Practice maintaining your low drama state while responding.

If you cannot think of anything else to say, here are a few low drama responses you can try:

• *You may be right.*

- *I get it.*
- *I see.*
- *I can tell you've been thinking about this a lot.*
- *I hadn't thought about that.*
- *My, you're the curious one today.*

People will say extravagant, outrageous things in order to succeed at pulling you in to their psycho-emotional state. Stay centered and neutral. Avoid adding emotional content and stay warm. Do not be played. You cannot appear hurt, insulted, miffed, offended, upset or befuddled. Recognize that getting emotional in any way will give your instigator an edge. Deny them this, but do it cordially.

Pocket Cards: Level; Low Drama; Be Direct; Stay Centered and Neutral; Be Boring

PART IV

LISTEN TO YOUR BODY

10

GROUND

You grow up the day you have your first real laugh at yourself.

— Ethel Barrymore

Walk as if your feet are kissing the Earth.

— Thich Nhat Hanh

When we are upset, it is as if our centers of gravity move from our bellies to the tops of our heads. We can feel ourselves becoming less stable.

A way to manage this tendency is to *Ground* ourselves. It relates to the practice of "returning to the center" in T'ai Chi. This chapter gives you exercises for grounding and centering your body, and for applying the psychological elements of grounding as well.

Stay Grounded and Cultivate Humility

The word "humility" and the word "humble" have at their root the Latin word for ground: humus.

Some think of being humble and showing humility as positive traits, whereas others believe that being humble means giving up dignity.

As we seek to apply it, cultivating humility does *not* mean losing dignity or self-respect, or that we have stopped listening to our own inner wisdom. We submit (pun intended) that humility is more about letting go of self-importance.

When we're too full of ourselves, convinced that we know what is best for everyone, or if we start to think that other people's opinions are not as important as our own, we have placed ourselves above our peers, and we have lost *ground*. In doing so, we interfere with our ability to connect with others and resolve things optimally.

When someone is "playing" us or pulling us into their system, we lose our center of gravity, our root, our connection to ground. When this happens physically, we can be easily controlled—when we are floating, we can be directed as easily as a feather. A similar thing can happen on a psycho-emotional level.

Staying grounded does not necessarily mean holding our ground in the traditional sense of digging in our heels with grim determination. What we really want is to stay with our center. That is our ground. The Soft Answer is about yielding and being gentle and unresisting, while not being controlled by others. One way we do this is by learning how to become and stay grounded.

When we are humble, we are being lowly in the highest sense. We are grounded. We are living in service to others. We are useful.

Getting Centered and Grounded

Practice developing an awareness of your own center of gravity. When you do these physical exercises, please be careful not to lock your knees or tense your back. Areas of excess tension can interfere with your connection to ground.

- Drop your awareness to your belly. Where is your center of gravity? Can you feel it?

- Physically, feel the ground. Relax and breathe to the bottom of your feet. Can you feel rooted?
- Pretend you are angry or agitated. Where is your center of gravity? Could you feel it change?
- Relax and breathe into your whole body. Does it feel as if your center of gravity has changed again?

Getting in touch with the physical sensations that go along with being grounded can be very helpful when you face a stressful situation of any kind.

In our language, there are clues to our innate understanding of the importance of sensing relationship to gravity and being grounded:

- Down to earth
- Upended
- Earthy
- Level headed
- Having a good foundation, a good base
- Uprooted; rooted; rooted out
- We get riled UP but we calm DOWN
- Take the legs out from under you
- Turn turtle
- Capsize

We use these phrases to describe emotional states, but notice how they also connote a physical component of ground.

Grounding in the Face of "You"

The use of the word "you" in a statement can be powerful, but it is a knife that can cut many ways. That means you have to be very careful when you use it. Learn the power of "you" and train yourself to use it skillfully.

Wisely used, the word "you" can help cool things down, perhaps turn around the mind of your dialogue partner, or help bring them back to ground:

- *You have a really interesting way of looking at the world.*
- *You think of the most surprising things.*

However, if there is even the slightest ember, use of the word "you" can fuel a fire. Especially when "you" is used with absolutes like "always" and "never," or words like "can't," "don't," "won't," "shouldn't"..., watch out! In this context, it is likely that "you" is being used to accuse and blame. If you find this happening in a conversation, it is critical that you *Stay Warm but Keep your Cool, Take Your Time*, and give the situation your total attention.

When you hear the word "you" coming out of your mouth or someone else's, be aware of the context and the consequences. When someone else starts using the word "you," consider it a red flag: it can be used to manipulate. There is a risk of being pulled into someone else's unhealthy system. It's time to take a breath. It's time to *ground*.

Pocket Cards: Cultivate Humility; Stay Grounded; Ground; Return to Your Center; Breathe to the Bottom of Your Feet

11

COME TO YOUR SENSES

Our hearts resonate at the same frequency as the earth and the universe. Therefore, we are all valuable instruments in the orchestration of the world and its harmony.

— SUZY KASSEM

Not the senses I have but what I do with them is my kingdom.

— HELEN KELLER

Metaphors and other figures of speech are often linked to our different physical senses, and it is not uncommon for us to show a sensory preference in our language. For example, we may say, "I *see* your point," using visual sensory imagery, or "I *hear* what you're saying," using auditory sensory imagery. These preferences can either clash or harmonize with other people's sensory preferences. In a conversation, when we match our own speech to someone else's sensory mode, we are communicating a subtle, but direct message that we are listening and responding specifically to that person.

Our ability to skillfully harmonize with another person's sense-centered language just might be the thing that turns a confrontational conversation into a cooperative one. If we aim to develop an awareness, facility and flexibility with sense-centered language, we can improve our chances of connecting and cooperating with others. The power of this technique is not about trying to convince or persuade, but rather a sincere desire to connect and cooperate with someone.

Matching Sensory Expressions

Your first step in matching sensory expressions is to tune in to the type of sense-centered language being used by your conversational partner. Once you notice one or more expressions related to a particular sense, you can throw a targeted metaphor or two into the conversation to match their sensory mode and see where that leads the conversation. Flexibility is a hallmark of this expertise. Being able to give up your own sense-centered language preference and use someone else's language preference, really costs you nothing, but the connection you make can make a big difference in the conversation.

Here are some examples of the way sense-centered preferences can be represented in someone's words:

Sight: *It's clear that... I see that... It looks like... From my perspective... He's got blinders on. I agree, you can't just close your eyes to that.*

Hearing: *I hear you. You're coming in loud and clear. Sounds good to me. Let me chime in here. That's music to my ears. A little voice tells me...*

Taste: *That just leaves a bad taste in my mouth. It's so close I can almost taste it. I just want to savor the moment. I relish the thought.*

Touch: *He has a very warm personality. Let's try to smooth things out. It's a touchy situation. She gets so prickly. That just rubs me the wrong way.*

Smell: *Something smells fishy here. I only caught a whiff of that. That*

stinks! He always uses such perfumy language. Ah, the sweet smell of
success.

Movement: *Let's walk through this together. That was such a moving*
speech. I need to find a way to pull her back in the boat. I'm with you. This
situation is off-balance. That makes my heart just soar.

Speech can also be neutral of sensory metaphor: "Interesting." "I
understand." "I'm aware of that." Elgin suggests that if you are unable
to match a sensory mode, it is best to stay neutral and use no sensory
mode at all (rather than clash).

Do you use a dominant sense mode? If so, how does it reflect the
way you perceive and respond to particular situations?

Here are some exercises that can help us become more accus-
tomed to recognizing and matching sensory modes:

Harmonizing the Senses

Find a willing partner and try on a sensory mode. Make sure both
partners have reviewed the kind of language that represents specific
sensory modes. One partner (the leader) picks a sensory mode and
starts a conversation without telling the other person which one they
have chosen, using language to convey that sensory mode. When the
other partner (the follower) recognizes that sensory mode, he or she
tries to match it.

If the leader uses sight-related terms, the follower should try
using sight metaphors in the conversation. Make sure to include a
few different expressions with the same sensory mode. Take turns
being the leader and the follower. If you cannot match the sensory
mode, try to use neutral language that does not invoke a competing
sense.

For a trickier exercise, practice deliberately varying your
sensory style—this might be harder than you think. The leader
starts a conversation in one sensory mode, and the follower
matches it. At some point, the leader choses a new sensory mode,

and the follower has to stick lightly by changing to the new sensory mode.

Discuss your experiences with these exercises. Was it easy to stick to one sensory mode? Was it easy to follow the sensory mode and still stay part of the conversation? This definitely takes practice. If it helps, try audio recording the practice conversation and listening to it together. There might have been some extra senses that slipped in without anybody noticing.

Your next step is to try sensory matching during friendly conversation when your partner does not know you are paying attention to sensory mode. As it gets easier for you to do this in comfortable conversations, applying this technique in more challenging situations will get easier as well.

Harmonizing Physically

The above technique and exercises can help you learn how to create harmony in terms of the sense-related words and phrases you use. It is also possible to develop your sense of social harmony so you can harmonize with others in broader ways.

Here is another, more physical way to harmonize:

Swimming Together Like Fish in a School: This is an exercise in mirroring. Stand next to each other, shoulder to shoulder. Your arm should be next to your partner's arm (for example, your left arm and your partner's right arm). Bend your elbows and point the fingers forward, but have your thumbs up so that you can wiggle your hands like swimming fish. Your forearms should now be parallel to each other. Keep about 3-4 inches of space between your arms.

One of you will lead while the other mirrors like a fish in a school, moving in the same direction and with the same speed. The leader walks around the room, and the other tries to "stick" and follow, so that both hands are moving like two fish swimming together, maintaining the 3-4 inch space between them. Next, switch who is leading and who is following.

For a variation, try doing this exercise while touching at the backs of the hands, or holding a sponge or a rubber ball or a small book between the backs of both of your hands or wrists.

Notice how, if you tighten up the muscles in your arm or deliberately harden your body someplace, success becomes more difficult to achieve: It is easier to stay connected and follow someone if we can *Relax*.

For an interesting challenge, try doing this with a partner with neither of you leading (which is the same as both of you leading), but with no talking. Just say "go," start moving, and see what happens.

Pocket Cards: Harmonize; Connect; Match a Sensory Mode; Stay Neutral

12

TAKE YOUR TIME

For fast acting relief, try slowing down.

— LILY TOMLIN

The hurrier I go, the behinder I get.

— GRANDMOTHER DIXON'S KITCHEN TRIVET

I n the classic TV show, *Columbo*, Peter Falk plays L.A. homicide detective Lt. Columbo who is a master at taking his time. In doing so, he is rewarded by having a chance to think things through.

When people are wound up, they usually want us to be wound up too. They want us on their time, in their state of urgency. But just because *they* are talking fast does not mean that we have to.

Take Your Time; Go Easy

If it is our turn to speak and if someone is waiting for our reply, we have every right to take all the time we need to formulate our response. We can nod our head. We can say, "I see." We can change our physical position in a way that indicates that we are thinking very carefully about whatever it is they are saying.

We do not have to rush to reply. We do not have to be pulled into the struggle. As Kat and Susan's father, Ron, used to say, "Go easy." *Take Your Time.*

This holds true in T'ai Chi as well. We don't lead, we follow. At first, that may not seem like this will get us where we want to go. We eventually learn that by following, when someone else makes a move, we can actually seem to arrive first.

Immunize yourself against false urgency. Recognize that, just because someone approaches you with a sense of urgency, this does not mean that the circumstances warrant swift action. If someone can make you experience a sense of urgency, they have tapped into and adjusted your emotional landscape; they are controlling you. Advertisers, conmen and salespeople use this tactic of trying to induce false urgency all the time. To avoid being pulled in; here are some responses to try:

- *Hmmm....I guess I'll have to think about that.*
- *Wow—that sounds interesting, but I'm not in a position to accept that kind of invitation right now.*
- *I have no idea how to answer that, but you've certainly given me a lot to think about.*

When slowing down, stay aware of the listener's perspective. We do not want to go so slow that it pushes someone to frustration or anger. That is not the point. We just want to stay sure-footed and aware.

So, nod, breathe, and *Take Your Time...Go Easy.*

Buy Time

Time creates space between a pugnacious statement and your considered, measured reply. You want to listen to your partner and be attentive, combining this with the practice of following, so that you can be appropriately and optimally responsive. Time is space; space is time.

Buy Time by creating space. Remember, a person who is trying to rush you, intentionally or not, is trying to control you. This gives you permission to respond in a way that preserves your own welfare. The techniques below are deliberate distractions, but they are harmless and friendly ones, never mean-spirited.

• **Drop something dispensable** (a napkin, pen, spoon, keys, etc). This buys you time and space. You can move to pick the item up, but even if the other person or someone else picks it up for you, the disruption and the related exchange will give you both a chance to pause, catch your breath, reconfigure, and consider changing your relative body positioning.

• **Excuse yourself momentarily**: "I'm sorry. I drank a ton of coffee earlier and I really have to use the bathroom. I do want to hear you out, and I'll be right back." "I really need to find a sip of water— would you excuse me for just a few moments?" You do not need to wait for their permission to leave; you have explained politely why you have to leave, so just quickly go. But, in these instances, remember to *be sincere*: don't say you will come right back if you have no intention of doing so.

The use of distractions can buy one time and opportunity, and can be done artfully, such as when a magician uses sleight of hand or when a red tassel at the hilt end of a T'ai Chi sword swirls around and distracts the eye of an opponent. Every schoolteacher worth his or her salt is skilled in the art of distraction and uses it for the overall benefit of the group. Used skillfully and responsibly, distraction can be a good thing, and a useful strategy to have in our toolkit.

Breathing, Time and Stamina

Breathing is related to time. It can help when you need a moment to slow down, to *take your time.*

Fuller, deeper, better breathing is associated in research studies with enhanced well-being, mood, attention, mental focus and stress tolerance. Relaxed, full breathing can lower blood pressure and regulate pH levels in the body. All these benefits start to occur almost immediately when you slow down and deepen your breathing.

When we get agitated, we sometimes hold our breath—we "forget" to breathe. Usually we don't even know it is happening. So, we take time to be very deliberate about our breathing.

This also expands on the concept that we want to *relax and listen internally*. If you are in the middle of a challenging social situation, remember to keep your breathing quiet, so it does not manifest as a sigh or a gasp.

Try to comfortably extend the length of your breath and see if you can keep your exhale longer than your inhale. You can do this by inhaling to a count of 5 and exhaling to a count of 7. Then, gradually increase the numbers.

The smart phone app *Breathe2Relax*, and similar programs teach awareness of your breathing and can help you slow it down. Many of these programs are free.

Taking your time and minding your breathing can also help with stamina. You have to pace yourself when you are in a challenging situation that may last for a while. The more relaxed you are, the longer you can stay present. You might also have noticed that the chance of having verbal difficulties increases when you or the person you are with is tired, so it is always a good idea to get enough rest. Even if you are fatigued, the more you have practiced managing your own breathing, the easier it is to deal with verbal difficulties.

Whenever possible, practice with easier situations and mini-confrontations that are less emotionally loaded.

Pocket Cards: Go Easy; Take Your Time; Buy Time; Breathe; Sl-o-o-o-w D-o-w-w-w-n

PART V

SYSTEMS

13

BOUNDARIES

I am not afraid of storms for I am learning how to sail my ship.

— Louisa May Alcott

...give me grace to accept with serenity
the things that cannot be changed,
Courage to change
the things which should be changed,
and the Wisdom to distinguish
the one from the other.

— Reinhold Niebuhr

When you are involved in a conversation, you are functioning as part of a system. A system is a group of connected components (in this case, people) that function as a whole. All members of the group have influence on the workings of the whole. This means that you, as one of the components of a group, have at least some sway. As the saying goes, "It takes two to tango."

Becoming Aware of Systems

Awareness of systems can help us reframe problematic human inter-actions. This section presents a few ideas to get started. We begin with two-person systems and the *Boundaries* that exist between any two individuals. Next, we will expand this to three-person systems (*Drama Triangles*), and finally larger groups (*Don't Kick the Dog!*).

When you are part of a dysfunctional system, understanding how it works can help you avoid negative outcomes. This goes back to the idea of learning how to *find the third option* beyond fight and flight. The interactive feedback loop of a verbal tussle gains energy if you push or if you pull, if you butt heads or if you shy away. Both fight and flight only serve to strengthen and reinforce the unhealthy aspects of the feedback loop.

So, what do you do? In order to influence a system, you have to stay part of it. Stay connected in a way that is light and loose, but full. Stick and remain part of the system, but not in such a rigidly coupled way that you get stuck and have no options for response. Under-standing how a system works can also help you extract yourself.

This is what makes the Soft Answer approach work. It is a system that applies to systems. Each action affects every other action and every component completely.

We are not trying to make the other person lose. We are trying to change the situation so that *no one loses*. Transform the game from being about winning (as in a win/lose game, also called a zero sum game) to being about creating a situation where both can receive benefit: win/win. Verbal T'ai Chi is a game changer.

Boundaries

The interface, or *Boundaries*, between two people is the most basic of interpersonal systems. This is where we begin our systems work. In order to recognize our role in any given interaction between ourselves and another, we have to be aware of boundaries.

Having healthy boundaries means we do not have a need to

control others and we do not allow them to control us. We take responsibility for our own actions and do not blame our actions on others (including a need to please or appease them). We respect others' needs for, and right to, privacy and agency. We do not apologize for our own need for the same.

When boundaries between two people become undefined and confused, the clarity of who has control over what gets blurry, and problems like enmeshment and codependency result. It is as if one person smells the pepper, but it is the other one who sneezes.

Boundary Busting

Almost all verbal attacks are attempts to pull you in to the other person's emotional system, a form of what we call boundary busting. An aggressor relies on your being emotionally invested, so that you can be controlled. Often this is done by instilling a sense of urgency of some kind. It is important to realize that whenever you are being unwittingly drawn in or pushed out (excited, agitated, annoyed, angered, insulted, scared...), you are being manipulated. It's time to clarify your boundaries.

An aggressor may be trying to control you, but you are not trying to control him or her in return. Rather, your goal, using as little effort as possible, is to remain part of the system so you can be a positive influence while at the same time avoiding being controlled by the other person in the system. In this way, you clarify the boundaries between you.

As you increase self awareness, awareness of others, awareness of the systems two or more people create (and become part of whenever they interact), you can also increase your confidence, effectiveness, and agency in being a part of any system. You will be creating a powerful, new and wonderfully effective skill-set for managing your part in the world.

It is possible that an aggressor is trying to intrude on your emotional territory unintentionally, out of a trained fear response, clumsiness or just bad habit. Whether intentional or unintentional, it does not matter to you, because either way, you are going to recognize the situation for what it is and remain centered, balanced, warm, and measured. If you can be responsive (vs. reactive), relaxed, aware and lightly connected, you can respond skillfully.

We urge you to learn about and respect healthy, appropriate boundaries, and to identify and manage boundary busting tactics like acting entitled, asking imposing questions, and being intrusive. What follows are a few exercises and strategies to help with this.

Take Your Sails Out of Their Wind

In a difficult conversation, the energy coming at you is like a stormy wind. Adjust yourself so that any negative energy is deflected away from you. In order to *Take Your Sails out of Their Wind,* you need to know who is the sailboat and who is the wind.

When we are the sailboat, we can change ourselves. We do not waste any time or energy complaining about the wind, trying to change it, or telling it what to do. We deal with it. We adjust and keep adjusting as necessary. In *Open the Book* we do this in a physical way, but we can do it conversationally as well. Part of developing your Soft Answer practice is discovering other ways to take your sails out of the other person's wind.

There are any number of ways that a person might overstep the bounds of polite conversation. Sometimes, people may give unsolicited advice about a situation that is none of their concern, or offer a comment or an opinion as a way of trying to get more information about a situation that is not their business. In these cases, offering a minimalist response can help to take your sails out of their wind. Here are some possibilities:

- *That's a thought.*
- *I wouldn't know.*
- *I'm sorry, I can't help you with that.*
- *I just couldn't say.*
- *I have no idea.*

- *Sounds like you have a lot to deal with.*

My Stuff, Your Stuff

Here is a simplified version of a thought exercise inspired by the outofthefog.net website. Just think, when you have the time and space to do so, of a person you typically have difficult conversations with. What is your stuff and what is theirs? Just think of your differing bodies, histories, experiences, ways of seeing the world, feelings, tastes and preferences (music, food, clothing, recreational activities), whatever comes to mind. This simple act can help you clarify your boundaries and may improve the foundation for your next exchange.

Umbrellas in a Windy Rain

Pay close attention the next time you are walking in the rain with an umbrella on a very windy day. How do you hold the umbrella?

Unless you point the umbrella directly into the wind, the wind will catch it and turn the umbrella inside out, and you are going to get awfully wet. So, you pay close attention, and when the wind shifts direction, you feel it in your hands and make an adjustment. *You* do not decide where to point the umbrella, you let the wind decide. To do anything else would be ludicrous. It is useless to fight against the wind, so we know not to even try. We manage the situation rather than trying to control things beyond our ability, and we get out when we can.

Games

Becoming aware of how simple phrases may be used in predictable, unproductive and emotionally manipulative conversational patterns can help you avoid being pulled into what Eric Berne (founder of psychology's *transactional analysis*) classified as a *game*.

Obviously, the field of transactional analysis is far beyond the scope of this book, but even a glimpse can be quite useful when it comes to verbal self-protection.

Eric Berne wrote *Games People Play* in 1964, and the game that first led him to his transactional analysis theory was, "Why Don't You— Yes But". Each game has a *con* (like a pitch), and a *payoff*. In the game, "Why Don't You—Yes But", one person enlists another into helping them solve a problem (the *con*), but to each suggested solution, their reply is always, "Yes, but...". It is a game, in part, because the initiator does not really *want* to solve the problem, she may just want to fill a need for attention (the *payoff*), and the continuing loop of "Why Don't You—Yes But" satisfies this need quite nicely.

Recognize that, when someone repeatedly says "Yes, but..." in a conversation, this person may be offering resistance to the situation, despite the fact that he or she is using the word "yes." There may be a game afoot!

From "Yes, but..." to "Yes, and..."

To begin to develop awareness of others engaging in "Why Don't You —Yes But," we can start with ourselves. It is helpful to remember that sometimes *we* are the ones who, perhaps involuntarily, increase the tension in a conversation by appearing to be oppositional ("Yes, but..."), even if our intention is one of collaboration. If you hear your-self saying "Yes, but..." recognize the resistance on your part. Try substituting "Yes, and..." and notice how different this feels.

This simple technique has two components, the "yes" and the "and". The "yes" is the connecting word; it demonstrates to our partner that we have no intention of either fighting or fleeing. The "and" provides the transition to an adjoining (rather than opposing) perspective and positions us shoulder to shoulder, conversationally speaking. When we say "Yes, and...," we are verbally connecting and collaborating with our partner just as we do when we physically *open the book*. This phrasing puts us both on the same side of the issue and allows us to introduce our ideas from this new standing.

Going deeper into this, if, at anytime in a conversation, you become aware that *the other person* is starting to say, "Yes, but..." more than once, take notice. You may be getting pulled into a game. Use your Soft Answer techniques. *Ground. Buy Time.* Try saying, "Yes, and..." or, just say, "Interesting."

A few other phrases can work this way as well, and we can use them interchangeably with "Yes, and...":

- *True; and also...*
- *Agreed; so maybe...*
- *Good point, and it leads me to wonder if...*
- *Yes, I see the problem.*

Allow for some space in the conversation, then offer your neutral comment, and just wait.

Get Help from a Friend

Practice with a friend. Tell your friend in advance that you are trying to create a new habit of saying "Yes, and..." rather than "Yes, but..." Start with a conversational topic that you'd both enjoy, but that has little potential for emotional territory, such as a book you have both read, or a movie or restaurant or concert you have been to together. Ask your friend's help in noticing whether, and how often, you say "Yes, but..." and thank him or her each time it is pointed out to you. Rephrase and jump back into the conversation.

Other resources:

For more about Eric Berne and *Games People Play*, see: Eric-Berne.com

"Yes, But"—The Evil Twin to "Yes, And" by Karen Hough, HuffingtonPost.com

The "Yes But" Syndrome; "Staying in Your Dysfunctional Comfort Zone,"

TheSuccessfulGrownup.com

Intimate Partners, Maggie Scarf, TheAtlantic.com

Mitchell Roth uses his Aikido training to illustrate his "Yes, and..."

strategy: first agree, then make a statement; from *Avoid Guilt Trips and Get What You Want with Mental Aikido*, Mitchell Roth, Mitchell-Roth.com

Pocket Cards: *Take Your Sails Out of Their Wind*; *Take Responsibility*; *Respect Healthy Boundaries*; *Adjust and Keep Adjusting as Necessary*; *My Stuff, Your Stuff*; *"Yes, and ..."*

14

DRAMA TRIANGLES

Every human being is entitled to courtesy and consideration. Constructive criticism is not only to be expected but sought.

— Margaret Chase Smith

Blame is not productive. Blame disguises and conceals. Blame alienates and separates. Blame is the killer of community, cooperation, and collaboration.

— Peter Rouse

O ld fish to two young fish as he swims past them: *"G'mornin' boys. How's the water?"*
Confused young fish to his friend after the old fish has swum past: "What's water?"

≈

Often, when we become acclimated to a system, we are not even aware we are in it. This can happen if we are pulled into a game, such as we saw in the previous section. Another system we may be recruited to participate in, identified by Stephen Karpman, is known as a *Drama Triangle*.

Karpman first wrote about drama triangles in 1968. The three corners of a drama triangle are the positions of the victim, the persecutor and the rescuer.

It is important to be clear about what a drama triangle is *not*. It is not a case of a thief (the persecutor) robbing a helpless person on the street (the victim) and a policewoman (the rescuer) intervening. Rather, it is a model for social exchanges, a set of enmeshed egocentric states people may learn, and then habitually (and some perhaps, deliberately) gravitate towards.

If we have learned this pattern inadvertently, we may slip into one of the three corners of the triangle unconsciously when we feel desperate or drained. The corner positions are characterized by high-drama behavior that can provide an energizing charge or a needed release.

For our purposes, you may regard a verbal aggressor as the persecutor, and the one being aggressed upon as the victim. Where is the rescuer? Well, here it gets a little complicated, because a drama triangle *may* have three people, but it can also have only two. A person who spends a lot of his or her life in a drama triangle framework often *switches between* the three positions; it's just that there is one corner of the triangle that is particularly comfortable for that person. It is also common for a person who tends toward a particular corner in one setting to move over to another corner in a different setting.

When we look at drama triangles in the context of a game, such as the "Why Don't You – Yes, But" scenario, the person who approaches with the problem takes on the role of the victim and the person who continually attempts to problem-solve is in the role of rescuer. Eventually, the rescuer may get sick of the endless loop and start to lose his or her temper. In this case, things can pivot, and the roles can flip on a dime. The rescuer may shift to the role of the victim or persecutor:

Why do you ask me to help when you don't really want it? You always do this to me! (victim)

Why are you always getting into trouble? Don't you ever learn? (persecutor)

...meanwhile, the person who began in the victim role may tire of hearing all these solutions, and may blurt out something like:

Ugh! You're never any help. I don't know why I even talk to you about these things! (transitioning to persecutor)

or...

You're supposed to be helping me, but all you do is criticize! (staying the victim, but moving the rescuer to the persecutor position)

Looking at Drama Triangles in an organizational framework, imagine Mary, a store manager. Elsa is her long-time assistant manager, but Mary really needs at least two assistant managers, and this is where Joe comes in.

Mary hires Joe, because she believes that Joe is going to come into the organization and solve all their problems. The main problem, as far as Mary is concerned, is Elsa. Mary is stuck with her, since legally, Elsa can't be fired unless she really messes up. Joe becomes the new darling in the office, and Mary cannot wait for him to straighten everything out (including Elsa). But, Joe is not empowered by Mary to actually do anything effective, because Mary wants everything very tightly controlled, and is not comfortable with others actually making decisions that will never be up to her standards.

Joe, receiving the mixed message of needing to fix problems, combined with the lack of agency to actually do so, is in a bit of a double bind. He feels blindsided when, instead of the initial praising he received from Mary, she starts complaining that he's not working out the way she thought he would. She lashes out at him because he's not doing anything he's supposed to be doing. Joe later learns that this has happened before. When Elsa was hired, she was in a similar position.

Can you see the triangle positions? Mary, who has a need to feel in control of everything around her, mostly hangs out in the perse-cutor position, but Joe had no idea of this when Mary hired him. At that time, Mary had placed herself in the victim position (beset by a non-functional organization and her poor relationship with Elsa), which put Joe in the rescuer position—saving the organization. From Mary's perspective, Elsa is in the persecutor's corner, since Elsa is the reason the organization is having problems. Sometimes Mary becomes the self-righteous rescuer: no one else can do anything properly, so she feels that, once again, she has to step in, since she is the only one who can fix a problem. This leaves Mary with one foot in the victim corner as well.

No surprise to those of us familiar with drama triangles, Joe later realizes that Mary had initially put Elsa in the rescuer position, telling Elsa when she hired her that the organization's real problem was Harry. And of course Harry was the one (as you may have already guessed) who Mary had originally hired to straighten things out. Now, Mary, taking the persecutor's corner, is lashing out at both Joe and Elsa while simultaneously positioning herself as a victim, first blaming Elsa and now Joe for her problems. Chances are she will be hiring another rescuer soon.

Mary is familiar and comfortable with the unhealthy drama triangle pattern; she will recruit others around her to take their places in the system. There is a good chance that Mary does this without even being aware of it.

WHAT CAUSES SOMEONE TO BECOME A SERIAL BUILDER OF DRAMA triangles? Often they have been bullied and that is how they learned the controlling, persecutor behavior. Familiar with all three corners of the triangle, they see the world through win/lose frameworks: rescue or be rescued, bully or be bullied, blame or be blamed. Even as they intimidate, for example, they can quickly jump to a victim or rescuer position for relief, because they cannot bear being the bully any longer, nor do they want to see themselves as part of the problem.

Why would someone ever choose to be a victim? Well, "choose" is complicated. Most people in the drama triangle structure are, like the young fish in the joke at the beginning of this chapter, clueless as to the very water they are swimming in. But, a key advantage to being in the victim position is a feeling of being blameless. The victim has done nothing wrong; they have done everything right. They cannot be blamed and they cannot be held responsible for their position. At its worst, victimhood is an infantilizing state, and sometimes a self-righteous one. The victim blames others readily, but cannot tolerate being blamed or held responsible.

How can you avoid ending up in a corner of a Drama Triangle? Be on the alert and pay attention. If you suddenly feel an urge to rescue, to blame, or if you begin to feel helpless, these are all red flags that a drama triangle may be starting to assemble in your midst. Stay relaxed and start to listen internally. Take your time and ground, and maintain a low drama position.

Tempted to rescue? Try applying compassionate detachment and offer encouragement: "That's unfortunate; but I guess if anybody can figure it out, you can."

Feeling compelled to blame? Instead, offer to listen deeply: "Maybe you could tell me more about that?"

Feeling collapsed or helpless? Try to buy time: "I think I need to take a step back and think about this."

As you learn how to recognize drama triangles and other problematic interpersonal structures, you will be improving your understanding of the kinds of sticky, energy-draining systems that can emerge in relationships, and may be able to short-circuit them before they get a chance to develop, and sometimes even avoid them completely.

Pocket Cards: Low Drama; Avoid Drama Triangles

15

DON'T KICK THE DOG!

One thing moves, everything moves.

— T'AI CHI CLASSICS

You take your life in your own hands, and what happens? A terrible thing, no one to blame.

— ERICA JONG

K ick the Dog is a system and a syndrome illustrated by a story which is all about misplaced aggression and blame. Become familiar with it in order to avoid it as much as possible. The story goes like this:

A man gets yelled at by his boss at work.

He can't yell at his boss or he will risk losing his job, so, when he gets home, he yells at his wife.

The wife, afraid of further angering her husband, in turn yells at the oldest child, who yells at the next oldest child, and so on, until now the youngest child is on the receiving end of the flak.

Having no one else to whom he can transfer the aggression, and lacking the skills to manage it any other way, the youngest child kicks the dog.

In a workplace with a *Kick the Dog* culture, a worker who can't solve a problem herself will be reluctant to take it to her supervisor. Since blame is constantly being passed down already—why invite more? This can be disastrous to a business or organization, and may be a coping strategy coming down from the very top. How is a problem supposed to get solved?

In a functional organization, just the opposite happens. When someone sees a problem, they have no hesitation to report it to the person above them. They know that they will not be yelled at or automatically blamed. The supervisor responds with gratitude. They *want* to know about problems as soon as possible so they can be taken care of quickly and easily, and before they grow into even bigger problems. If the one who reports the problem and the supervisor cannot solve the problem together, the two do not hesitate to take it to the next person up the ladder, who in turn responds with gratitude and joins the problem-solving team.

This is one of the main differences between a healthy and an unhealthy organization. *Kick the dog* cultures pass blame down the hierarchical ladder, which obstructs problem solving. Healthy, functional organizational cultures encourage identifying problems and move them up the ladder as needed, so they can be addressed efficiently and effectively.

The *kick the dog* mentality stems from displaced anger and the viral nature of aggressive behavior. The hostility is passed along mindlessly. Very often, blame ("playing the blame game") is passed along with it. In The Soft Answer credo, we *don't kick the dog* and we *Don't Play the Blame Game*. Instead, we recognize that when we blame others, it is as if we are saying that they have control over our lives. In doing this *we place ourselves* in the victim position, disempowering ourselves and ceding power to others.

You may have noticed how unhelpful patterns can spread and persist in any organization, from a small family or club to a huge corporation or social group. For example, currently, there is a popular concept that we need to protect ourselves against what are labeled "toxic people" and "toxic companies." This is a form of blaming, and it is almost certainly a simplistic characterization. Instead, consider that perhaps it is not the people or the organizations that are toxic, but the habits and patterns that have been learned and are reflexively passed along.

Aggression and blaming are often motivated by fear and can be contagious. According to a 2009 study by Nathanael J. Fast of USC Marshall School of Business and Larissa Tiedens of Stanford University entitled *Blame Contagion: The Automatic Transmission of Self-Serving Attributions*, "the goal of protecting one's self-image (embedded in the act of blaming others for one's failures), is socially contagious."

If you think that your own status and self-image increases if you decrease the status of another, you have bought into the zero sum game idea we mentioned earlier: in order for someone to win, someone else has to lose. And, if you believe that someone else having control or power means that you must have none, you are stuck in the same win/lose belief system. It's just that now you are on the other end of the spectrum. This is one way to look at the phenomenon of *Learned Helplessness*.

Learned Helplessness

In 1967, Dr. Martin Seligman first observed and began to formulate his theory of *Learned Helplessness*. When creatures (such as ourselves) have repeated experiences in which nothing they do results in their circumstances improving, they can learn helplessness. The condition is so debilitating that, even when the situation changes and their ability to change what is happening around them is restored, they still cannot take action.

If we believe that nothing we do can have a positive influence in a situation (if we feel like we are the "dog" that is always being kicked or the one who is always being blamed), we may develop a kind of "learned helpless" state where that situation is concerned.

Are there antidotes to *kick the dog, the blame game* and *learned helplessness?* Fortunately, yes. Behaving cheerfully and responsibly can also be contagious in an organization or interpersonal system, and Seligman found that those who have learned to be helpless can be trained to take appropriate effective action, and that, in time, their sense of agency can be restored.

More recently Seligman's work has focused on positive psychology, Authentic Happiness, Authentic Humility, and Well-being Theory. We highly recommend you investigate his work, which may be found at authentichappiness.sas.upenn.edu

Be a Positive Influence

We can commit to liberating ourselves from the disempowering shackles of blame, aggression, and helplessness and become agents of positive change in our world by deliberately cultivating and compassionately embodying courage, joy, self-control and responsibility.

The saying from the T'ai Chi classics, "One thing moves, everything moves," is a recognition of the interconnectedness of all things. Notice how you are a member of many larger groups and systems: family, work, school, friends, church, book club, lefties, dancers, speakers of English, etc. These are all groups on which you can have a beneficial influence just by introducing small, positive changes.

In his *Peace Class*, Colman McCarthy, author of *I'd Rather Teach Peace,* assigns for homework the following exercise: do something for someone without them knowing about it and for which you cannot be repaid. This is an example of "paying it forward," and it is very powerful. Try it and you may be surprised to learn the positive effects of this simple practice.

What else can you do to positively influence the people and groups with whom you interact daily?

If you have a tendency to unconsciously and readily blame others or to accept misplaced blame from others (and almost all of us do at some time), begin to actively train yourself to resist that temptation.

Try building in even a little space between your impulse to act and your actions. Breathe, suspend judgment, inhibit reactions, and let it go.

Pocket Cards: Don't Kick the Dog!; Don't Play the Blame Game; Solve Problems Together; Suspend Judgment; Be a Positive Influence; Let it Go!

PART VI

PITFALLS

16

DON'T TAKE THE BAIT!

Defense is the beginning of war.

— JAMES DODD

We should strive, not only to say the right thing in the right place, but far more difficult, to leave unsaid the wrong thing at the tempting moment.

— LADY DOROTHY NEVILL

S uzette Haden Elgin taught the maxim "Don't take the bait." She came up with insightful, extensive linguistic analysis on how to identify when we are being baited in conversation. We highly recommend taking a look at Elgin's work. This is wide and deep territory, with nearly endless aspects, so this chapter is necessarily an introduction to the concept. Let's begin.

Locate the Bait

Have you ever come away from an encounter feeling hoodwinked, blindsided, frustrated, defeated, overwhelmed, confused, disoriented, or angry?

It may be that you were baited and you got hooked. Bait can take the form of a comment, a question, or even a tone of voice. Bait is something unexpected that suddenly comes across our path, and prompts a reaction in us which results in a significant and detrimental change in our circumstances.

When we inadvertently take the bait, we may find ourselves mulling over the details of what happened, rehashing what was said, trying to figure out who was more right and who was more wrong, or trying to justify our actions. None of this gets to the root of the problem, which is that someone offered bait and we took it because we didn't recognize it.

When we fall for the "con" and take the bait (and we all do from time to time), we are pulled into a kind of reality distortion field of emotional reflexes. We may not wake up to what has happened until the payoff that the other person was searching for has been achieved. We may not come back to thoughtful deliberate action until our reflexive reactions have run their course.

Falling for conversational bait will bring you to a place where you did not expect to be. You might have gotten into an argument you did not anticipate, or you might be doing a favor for which you feel resentment or regret or discomfort. If you can complete the sentence: 'All of a sudden, I found myself..." with something like:

- *...resentfully driving two hours out of my way*
- *...caught in the middle*
- *...yelling and losing my temper*

...odds are, you took 'the bait.'
If you find this happening, ask yourself:

- *How did this start?*
- *Where did this start?*
- *When did this start?*

If you have trouble answering these questions, imagine telling your story to a friend. Where would you begin?

As we become more adept at recognizing bait, we are better able to reflect on these conversational events and figure out how we could have seen the bait for what it really was. Over time, we develop a more helpful set of reflexes. Be gentle and forgiving with yourself. This is not easy stuff: there are years of embedded reflexes to re-train!

Tuning into the Feeling of Being Baited

If you can develop a sensitivity to "bait," you can most easily influence the course of the conversation. It may be useful to recall an episode in which you were successfully "hooked." You can go back over it and see if you can tell when the clues started to emerge. In a bait situation, you may experience the following:

- Feeling pulled in
- Feeling a need you didn't have before this encounter began
- Sensing a shift in your emotional landscape
- Noticing that the drama level is increasing
- An urgency has been triggered in you
- A dissonance between what the other person is saying and how you're feeling (unsettled and disoriented)
- Feeling compelled to engage in fight/persecutor, flight/victim or rescue actions
- Blaming, name-calling or labeling

If you feel like there is even a remote possibility that someone has thrown a baited hook in your direction, tune in to your senses. Are you feeling an emotional response? An emotional response can resonate all through you. Respect and pay attention to this signal. If you are too quick with a reflexive response, that is a red flag that you may be responding to bait.

Ask yourself:

- *Do I feel it in my head?*
- *Do I have a "gut feeling"?*
- *Do I feel a "knowing" in my "heart of hearts"?*
- *Do I have some of each of these feelings?*
- *Do I feel conflicting signals, either inside myself, coming from the other person, or between the two of us?*

If someone is putting something forth as being a rational conclusion, position, or request, but you're feeling an emotional component bubbling up in your urge to respond, or a "tempting moment" (as Lady Dorothy Nevill calls it), this is a clue that a hook may be lurking beneath some bait.

When these feelings arise, remember that you have already learned something about how to frame and manage them:

- If you feel pulled in, remember: *Compassionate Detachment.*
- If you feel a need that you did not have before this encounter began, remember: *Pay Attention.*
- If you feel a shift in your emotional landscape, remember: *Relax and Listen Internally.*
- If you feel that the drama level is increasing, remember: *Low Drama.*
- If an urgency has been triggered in you, remember: *Take Your Time.*
- If you feel a dissonance between what the other person is saying and how you're feeling, remember: *Ground.*
- If you feel compelled to engage in flight/persecutor, flight/victim or rescue actions, remember: *Recognize Drama Triangles.*
- If it starts to feel like it's about you, not them (a boundary busting alert message), remember: *Boundaries.*
- If blaming is involved, remember: *Don't Kick the Dog!*

You can only avoid taking the bait if you learn how to sense it before you are lured in.

So, listen to your body, and tune into the feeling of being baited. You will be developing the skill of getting attuned to the sensations that accompany being baited, and installing your own internal early warning system.

What if the anxious emotional reaction you are having is in response to someone's completely sincere and innocuous comment or question and not a bait statement? The thoughtful actions we describe in the next section will work equally well in either case to protect and *Ground* you.

Thoughtful Action in Response to Bait

You have begun to recognize bait. You have begun to recognize your physical and emotional responses to bait. Now what?

Understand that you cannot control whether someone puts out bait for you. You can only control how you respond to it.

Your mission is to avoid taking the bait, thereby short-circuiting a chain of events that makes you vulnerable to covert manipulation, whether it is deliberate or unintended. What kind of response can you give that allows you to avoid taking the bait?

Recognizing the physical manifestations of the emotional trigger is a start. If, at the beginning of the bait sequence, you can lead the conversation in a different direction, you may open a space for change.

There are several ways to accomplish this. Your response will differ depending on the level of engagement you choose to bear in the particular relationship. You can try some of these ideas:

Sympathize, but don't patronize: *That's got to be difficult.*

Clarify your boundaries, but with kindness: *It sounds like you've got a lot going on right now.*

Agree with what you can: *It's true that we haven't gone to the movies together in a very long time. It was great having that much free time.*

Be a little tedious and long-winded: You would not do this deliberately in a friendly conversation, but if you are in danger of being baited, being a bit leaden and tiresome, (though of course still sincere and respectful), is fair play. And even if you have guessed wrong, there's no harm done.

Buy time: *It's obvious that this is important to you. Let's set aside a time when we can focus on it exclusively.* Respond this way only if you plan to do so.

Solve problems cooperatively: *Let's ask Mary. She's great at this stuff.* If some part of the problem at hand does involve you, you can propose seeking a solution together, preferably with a third party who can offer a helpful perspective.

Own up: *You're right, I should have put the applesauce away before I went to bed. I'm sorry about that.* If you are in the wrong, admit it, fix what you can, and move on with a matter-of-fact attitude.

Remember, you want to reroute any of your own unhelpful emotional reflexes so that you can clear a new path, keep yourself safe from being baited, and allow the other person a graceful way out of an unattractive behavior pattern (trying to bait you in the first place).

The good news is (as Elgin teaches), that you can learn to locate the bait before you develop the more advanced skill of identifying the bait's underlying presuppositions. You can respond to baited hooks without ever discerning exactly what the hook is or what the person "fishing" is trying to get you to do. In fact, you can even do this if you are not completely sure about whether you're being baited or not.

A skillful response allows your conversational partner a gracious way out, if he chooses to take it, but it also lets a deliberate fisherman know that his baited hook is not going to work with you.

Always be gentle with yourself; stay mindful and steady.

Pocket Cards: Locate the Bait; Don't Take the Bait!; "All of a sudden I found myself..."

17

STEER CLEAR OF JADE

Against criticism a man can neither protest nor defend himself; he must act in spite of it, and then it will gradually yield to him.

— JOHANN WOLFGANG VON GOETHE

Never explain—your friends do not need it and your enemies will not believe you anyway.

— ELBERT HUBBARD

J ADE stands for Justify, Argue, Defend and Explain. Typically, we find ourselves resorting to JADE tactics after we have taken the bait on the hook. We do not always recognize bait before we have fallen into the trap, so when we find ourselves Justifying, Arguing, Defending or Explaining, we should consider that we may have taken the bait.

Neutralize

If we find JADE manifesting in a conversation, we can cultivate unaffected neutrality. JADE cannot easily survive in an emotionally neutral environment, so presenting a neutral demeanor can take an exchange out of JADE mode.

Neutralizing means using responses that are dispassionate, detached, and present. They are unassertive, unruffled, composed, self-possessed, untroubled, unperturbed, yet poised:

- *Ah...*
- *Why does anyone ever do something like that?*
- *I suppose there could be hundreds of answers to a question like that.*
- *I'm not sure how to answer that, but you're certainly pointing out something I hadn't thought of.*
- *That's quite a question.*
- *That's very interesting. I'm not sure I'd ever think to ask a question like that.*

In some cases, we can respond neutrally, and then quickly change the subject:

> A: What's it going to take for you to get that car of
> yours cleaned?
> B: I'm not really sure—Hey, did you watch the game
> yesterday?

Of course we know some people who will not be deterred—they will come right back with that first accusation, or a variation of it, over and over again. When this happens, you may want to try combining strategies. Use anything and everything in your Soft Answer skill set to avoid wasting your time or energy Justifying, Arguing, Defending or Explaining, and do your best to cultivate unaffected neutrality.

You may be thinking that if we respond neutrally, we are allowing a would-be bully to "get away with it." Not so. Justifying, Arguing, Defending and Explaining are all signs that we are participating in the quarrel. Remember, the way the would-be bully "wins" is by getting us to react, to fight, or to run away. By staying neutral, we are doing neither of these, and we may be opening a space for a win-win outcome as well.

Observe People Using JADE Tactics

Spend part of a day just observing how much energy and time people waste when they are:

- Justifying their actions to an accuser whose mind is made up
- Arguing with someone whose mind is not about to change
- Defending themselves (i.e., getting defensive)
- Explaining their position to someone who just is not going to listen.

Try to identify bait and JADE responses in a movie or a TV show. Look for unaffected neutrality as well. What other responses work or don't work? You may want to write down some of these in your Soft Answer notebook.

More on Blame

As we saw in *Don't Kick the Dog!*, blame is a time and energy waster. Usually, it is a bad habit we have picked up along the way.

Blaming is different from holding someone responsible. If I hit somebody's car with my own, I need to take responsibility. What we are talking about here is blame that is used as an emotional crutch, an escape or excuse to avoid responsibility or complicity. A person might think, if he can successfully pin the blame on someone else, he is absolved. In other words, he assigns blame in order to try to remain blameless. For this reason, there are people who will exhaust themselves in order to find others they can blame.

If we suddenly see a broken glass on the floor and no one else is around (maybe there was an earthquake, maybe the cat knocked it over), most likely we would clean it up without a second thought and have a fairly neutral emotional reaction.

But what if two people are home? Imagine one gets a phone call, and in going for the phone, puts a glass down in a precarious place. Then the other person comes in, does not see the glass, knocks it over, and it breaks.

There are some people, given this situation, who would each, without thinking, apologize to the other for their part, and then would quickly clean up the glass and move on.

On the other end of the spectrum, there are others who, with a desperate need to avoid responsibility, could waste several minutes arguing about who is to blame, and why the other person should clean up. Given enough stubbornness, they might both walk away, leaving the broken glass on the floor as a dare to see who would cave-in first.

This is a power-play. It is emotionally loaded behavior that robs us of our functionality. It is a waste of time and energy. No one wins; both lose.

SOMETIMES A PROBLEM ARISES BETWEEN PEOPLE FROM OPPOSITE ENDS of the functionality spectrum; then what happens? A skillful person will not allow themselves to be brought into an emotional power struggle: They will not take the bait. They might level with the other person: "It would be a shame if someone got cut. Why don't we clean it up together?" If the emotionally volatile person is accusatory and says they are not cleaning it up, simply disregard any emotionally-loaded comments, recognize that, the other person is not in an emotionally stable place at the moment, remain neutral (neutralize), get the job done, and move on.

Does this mean we allow ourselves to be taken advantage of? No. It is a matter of realizing that it is *better for us* to move on rather than hang on to an argument that no one can win.

What if we cannot imagine cleaning up the mess without feeling bitterness and resentment? It may be time for some self-reflection, *compassionate detachment* and forgiveness.

Bitterness and resentment can eat away at us from the inside. The ability to let go and move on is not a sign of weakness. It is actually very powerful.

This hearkens back to the concept of leaving the possibility for change open. Even if we do not get an immediate result, we have made it possible for a scenario other than lose/lose to arise, now or some time in the future, and the possibility of win/win is still on the table.

Pocket Cards: Steer Clear of JADE; Neutralize

18

MANAGING SNEAK ATTACKS

Peace is not the absence of conflict, but the ability to cope with conflict by peaceful means.

— Ronald Wilson Reagan

When they go low, we go high.

— Michelle Obama

Hen we feel ambushed, we tend to react. Whatever defensive habits are most deeply rooted emerge before we know it. Practice helps to dislodge unhelpful habits and allows new coping mechanisms to take root in their place. If you are the target of a sneak attack, take a step back, allow for some space, and offer the would-be attacker a graceful way out. It is likely that the attack is happening out of their own automatic reactions and habits.

Some spoken offensives will be boundary-busting, importuning, inappropriate questions. Others may be absolutist declarations or unreasonable requests. When someone tries to define, characterize or assign motives to you, or you hear pronouncements like "You always...," and "You never...," or comments that begin with "Don't you ever...," "You're such a...," or "Can't you just once...," ask yourself, "Am I being set up?" Then tread carefully, and see what you can do to create space.

Bear in mind that sneak attacks can work both ways. Particularly if you are learning The Soft Answer Verbal T'ai Chi system with a friend or partner, keep careful watch over your two different roles (partner/friend and Soft Answer support team member), lest they come into conflict at some point.

Suppose you notice that your friend has fallen back into a careless and unkind habit. Proceed thoughtfully. You will want to take great care in moments of increased strain (which are part of the natural rhythm of all intimate relationships), to resist urges to indict the person by blurting out something like, "I thought you were supposed to be learning how to handle this kind of thing—where's your soft answer now?" It is tempting, and may even feel temporarily satisfying to deliver a clever quip, but it is counter-productive and is not part of a Soft Answer practice.

"Let's Take a Step Back"

Whether the other person is intending to be difficult or not, we can create space and give them a chance to find a gracious way out by proposing, "Let's take a step back."

Another way to put this: Be kind, rewind.

We can ask to go back to an earlier point in the exchange and start afresh from there—if asked for a reason, we can say we just really want to make sure we understand exactly what the other person is saying. For example:

- *Before we go on, can we go back to an earlier point you were making? I want to make sure I understand it correctly.*
- *Let's rewind for a second, may we? I'm interested in hearing more about...*

Being able to step back, or to rewind and offer another chance, is an action that involves being able to forgive whatever transgression has occurred and moving past it so that you can go forward together. In *compassionate detachment*, we discussed being able to forgive yourself; can you also extend this generosity to others?

Using Platitudes

Platitudes are unexciting statements that do not really take a conversation forward. They are dull and may even be boring; the meaning of the root of the word *platitude* is the same as for *plate* and *platter*: flat.

Because of this quality, some believe platitudes have no place in conversation, but when we are dealing with a sneak attack, this is exactly what we want. With a "flat" comment we can stay in the conversation without contributing to its unfriendly direction and without supplying any emotional fuel.

Here are a few incendiary remarks to get you started, followed by a platitude or two you could use:

Remark: *You never do anything right!*
Platitude: *Well, you win some; you lose some.*
Platitude: *Such is life.*
Platitude: *You never know.*

Remark: *You're not having trouble with money again, are you?*
Platitude: *After a storm, the sun is bound to shine again.*
Platitude: *It's always darkest just before the dawn.*

Remark: *When will you ever learn?*
Platitude: *Time will tell.*
Platitude: *Tomorrow is another day.*

Give Others a Graceful Way Out

Develop the habit of being gracious and giving others a graceful way out when they misstep.

Start small and in the easy places. When people bumble or blurt, and the situation is generally low key and low pressure, try to figure out how to forgive them. Forgiveness is a nice thing to do for others, but we also do this for ourselves as well—it hurts *us* to hold on to anger and resentment.

Mix it Up

Try using a combination of techniques. In addition to asking to take a step back, you can make a simple and honest statement, starting with "As you know..." or using platitudes. Respond skillfully and generously and not aggressively to unexpected awkward comments such that your would-be importunist has a chance to reconsider.

If you have been collecting verbal tirades and tongue-lashings in a *Hot Buttons* section of your Soft Answer notebook, now is the time to bring them out to play. Likewise, if you have been building a collection of *Favorite Strategies* (Soft Answer responses that are a particularly good fit for you), now is the time to try them out.

Work with a friend or group if you can. One person delivers the attacks, the other practices responding, then switch. If you are lucky enough to be doing this with a group, get feedback from the observers. If not, you can always make audio or video recordings, and then review them together.

Developing Confidence: Now, Voyager

For further exploration of sneak attacks, watch the movie *Now, Voyager* (a wonderful ugly duckling story). The film offers a host of Soft Answer learning opportunities. In it, Bette Davis' character Charlotte has a boundary-busting mother who is a master of verbal control and manipulation. Charlotte also has a young niece, June, who has learned the family habit of poking fun at Aunt Charlotte.

Observe how the mother is deliberate and calculated in her verbal attacks. At the opposite end of the spectrum, Charlotte's niece, the naive June, says hurtful things to Charlotte, parroting her elders to join in the game, merely because it is part of the sport she has learned. The movie also has plenty of characters who are somewhere in between—blurters who let less-than-kind things come out of their mouths, almost uncontrollably.

Charlotte goes from being an intimidated wreck at the beginning of the movie to someone who can respond to her mother's bossiness calmly and effectively. As others around her stumble and make their gaffes, the now-skilled Charlotte gives them the space, and the opportunity, to modify their behavior.

Some people who use sneak attacks are being predatory and manipulative, but others are just being socially clumsy, awkward, nervous or taunting out of learned behavior and habit. As we said in *Boundaries*, we are not trying to play games with people; however, if people are playing games with us, we need to recognize this in order to respond appropriately.

We can be compassionate, kind and polite without being pushovers, and we can be perfectly nice without allowing ourselves to be stepped on.

By practicing, we can develop and maintain the confidence to be able to respond optimally for the given situation. Work from where you are. These are not simple things and each of us has to figure out for ourselves when, how, and how much to apply a given technique.

Pocket Cards: Be Kind, Rewind; "Let's take a step back"; Provide a graceful way out; Use Platitudes

PART VII

CHANGE

19

BOTH SIDES NOW

First seek to understand, then to be understood.

— ANONYMOUS

Spread love everywhere you go. Let no one ever come to you without leaving happier.

— MOTHER THERESA

In order to practice compassion, it is helpful to see things from the other person's perspective. As we have said from the beginning, everyone deserves to have their dignity and self-respect preserved. That is really the only way to have genuine communication. The majority of interpersonal conflicts are due to fear and misunderstanding. If we can step back and ask ourselves, "How might this look from the other side?" we might direct the interaction toward resolution.

Validate First

Validating allows us to confirm what our conversational partner is saying before we jump in with a reply. This puts us in a less threatening, more supportive position, which may take the edge off of a challenging exchange. We can use the question, "Are you saying...," and then restate our understanding of the other person's perspective, without judgment or comment.

We do not worry about looking two-faced by appearing to agree with something we do not like. That is not what is happening. We are simply acknowledging that this person is saying and thinking what they seem to be saying and thinking. If we have it right, our colleague will feel listened to, and if we have it wrong, this is very valuable to learn. We are going to graciously and generously give the other person another chance to get her message across.

The technique of *Validating First* dovetails nicely with an approach for managing difficult conversations originated by George Armitage Miller (a psychologist and a founder of the field of cognitive psychology). To apply *Miller's Law*, assume what the other person is saying is true, and try to imagine how it could be true.

Some people intentionally lie and deceive, but most do not. Whether they believe what they are saying is true or not, applying *Validate First* and *Miller's Law* can effectively provide a small shift in the direction of the conversation. In almost all cases, the response will be pleasantly unexpected.

Getting Perspective

This is a group exercise; solo and partner variations appear below.

Stand in a circle with your Soft Answer system peers. Now turn around, so that you are all facing outside the circle. One by one, share what it is that you are seeing in front of you (the clock, the door, the window). When everyone has finished, you, as the facilitator, can ask the group:

- We are all in the same room, do we agree? (Yes)
- Were all of our answers the same? (No)
- Was anyone lying, or trying to be deceptive or misleading? (No)

This illustrates that, despite everyone being in the same place at the same time, we can have varying yet valid perspectives.

Variations: This exercise can be done with as few as two people, or even alone. With a partner, just stand back to back and compare notes. If alone, stand in a room alone and turn yourself around slowly. You are in the same place, but your perspective is continually changing.

Take this idea into daily life: How often can you take someone else's perspective into account before you make a decision or take action?

Developing a Wider Pool of Resources

It is our hope that *The Soft Answer Verbal T'ai Chi* will be your gateway to the hundreds, if not thousands of other resources. Here's a start:

- *New Line Ideas,* a customer service training organization, offers several resources in the Learning section of their website that we find to be Soft Answer compatible. The technique they share called "fogging" involves validating the position of the person you are having a discussion with, so that things can go forward more smoothly: newlineideas.com
- In the article, *7 Tips for Resolving Conflicts Quickly and Peacefully,* Stephen Hopson recommends the technique of saying "Yes, yes, I see exactly what you're saying. You mean…" He also suggests taking the other person's perspective, and other valuable techniques. The article is posted at the self-improvement website, *Pick The Brain*: pickthebrain.com

- The Edmunds Community College counseling center website offers a conflict resolution guide from helpguide.org, and the HelpGuide site offers extensive similar resources, such as edcc.edu
- Myra Golden teaches customer service representatives how to manage difficult customers, but her Soft Answer-compatible techniques can often be applied to daily life: myragolden.com

Pocket Cards: Validate First; Seek to Understand; Apply Miller's Law; Get Perspective

20

RECONFIGURE

When you're through changing, you're through.

— Martha Stewart

Live your life receptively, like a willow in the wind.

— Thomas Moore

W hen things get difficult in a verbal transaction, we may suddenly feel trapped or stuck. The essence of being stuck is that we feel like nothing can move. Maybe we can't talk. We may hardly feel able to breathe. Our muscles might seize up. We may feel stuck inside our current posture. Our mind may feel as if it has stopped as well. Stress impedes our ability to even think.

When we *Reconfigure*, we are able to move and change: our bodies, our body language, our vocal tone, our breathing, our expression, even our thinking.

As we have previously discussed, a person aggressing has an innate understanding of how important connection is. They know experientially that in order for them to make their offensive work they need someone to offend. It takes two to tango. Thus, they are very motivated to stay connected.

But we can choose *how we participate* in that connection.

For example, if we are joyful, even if the other person wants to be grumpy and hard, they will know somewhere inside that they have to soften up a bit in order to stay connected with us. They will sense how an extreme mismatch will not work for them, will not help them achieve their goal. No matter how hard they originally planned to be, they will know that in the face of soft, open joy they will not have a way in.

When meeting difficulty or resistance, we imagine that we have the supple flexibility of bamboo, a new leaf, or a blade of grass underfoot that springs back up after it has been stepped upon. We *reconfigure.*

We remain connected in some way with our associate, and stay with the conversation if we can. We cultivate a quality of just being present: able to stick softly and lightly with the other person. Rather than initiating, we see if we can let her lead the exchange. As in T'ai chi, we are cultivating the skill of following their incoming energy, but gently redirecting it through our soft, full connection. Being able to *reconfigure* means being consciously and actively responsive.

If, along the way, we chose the wrong move, if we miscalculate, which happens to all of us at some point, no matter how practiced we are, there's no problem. We simply adapt: we readjust, recalculate, *reconfigure.* We do not keep using the same tactic if it is not effective for the situation. Pay attention to the changing environment respond to it.

Practice Reconfiguring

Bat a Balloon Around: Try batting a balloon around. You have to pay close attention to the balloon and its movement, as well as to your surroundings. You must constantly adapt and reconfigure according to your environment and to how the balloon responds. You can do this yourself, but it is also fun, and different, to do it with a partner, or even a larger group. Notice how your ability to attend and respond must expand and extend to your partners.

Shift Your Weight: Remember *Open the Book*? We shifted our weight and turned our bodies in order to have a different physical orientation to our aggressor: shoulder to shoulder rather than face-to-face. Sometimes simply shifting weight a bit or making a slight turn during a conversation can make a difference. Give it a try.

Copy Body Language: When you are in a crowd, take advantage of the situation and watch other people. Imagine copying their body language, expression or gestures. Tune in to others. How do they manage their hands? As they change their bodies, what else changes? Try to get a feel for the actions of others. You can also do this while watching television. Take the stances and copy the expressions and the body language of the people on TV. Keep reconfiguring. What do you notice?

Tune in to Volume: Changing your volume can provide a change of tune and tone when you are in a tough situation. Practice this by starting a conversation with a friend and using a slightly higher than usual voice volume. Have them respond with a slightly lower volume, and as you continue the conversation, notice how mismatched it feels when two people maintain very different volumes during a conversation. What happens? Adjust your volume and stay in tune with any impulses you have to make a change in either direction. Notice how difficult it is *not* to instinctively match your partner and bring things into concordance.

When things start heating up in a conversation, we want to avoid getting pulled in to using a higher volume. If we can stay attuned to the volume of our conversational partner and meet it at a slightly lower volume level, we may be able to subtly lead our partner to a lower volume, and thereby lower the tension.

Be sure to remain audible whether in practice or in an actual conversation. You want the other person to hear you. Remember that you are not trying to frustrate someone by lowering your voice so far that he or she cannot hear you and you are not trying to be manipulative or appear critical by making someone strain to hear you.

Stay Connected and Compassionate, But Stay Comfortable Too

There are those who are so used to being argumentative that they do not seem to easily give it up for a peaceable alternative. Perhaps for them, bickering and being disagreeable provides a special kind of charge, a stimulating shot of energy that helps them manage a restlessness, discomfort or just boredom. These people may not even be aware of their compulsive need to quarrel.

Have compassion for a person who is stuck in this need-loop. Stay with them when you comfortably can or must, offering them a graceful alternative to arguing when possible. Use your Soft Answer skills to stick lightly and be flexible and responsive. Sometimes when we *reconfigure*, it frees our partner to make a change as well.

Listen to your body and stay comfortable, and learn to recognize your approaching limits well before you reach them, and to *reconfigure* accordingly. Remember *compassionate detachment* and the "poor thing" perspective. Avoid exhausting yourself.

No effort succeeds one hundred percent of the time. If things are not going well, bow out gracefully, preferably early enough that you aren't feeling depleted.

You always have next time.

Pocket Cards: Reconfigure; No Insistence, No Resistance; Spring Back Up; Readjust; Stay Comfortable

21

REFLEXIVE KINDNESS

Three things in human life are important. The first is to be kind. The second is to be kind. And the third is to be kind.

— HENRY JAMES

When you forgive, you heal your own anger and hurt and are able to let love lead again. It's like spring cleaning for your heart.

— MARCI SHIMOFF

How can we develop a reflex of kindness? Practice. Actively practice being kind, positive, and cheerful. How can we get to kindness? We can *reconfigure*, be responsive, try new things. Kindness is the ground from which we act, and much like forgiveness, when we extend it to others, it is beneficial to us as well.

By actively cultivating kindness, we can move with a light heart and the confidence that we are coming from an open place, allowing solutions we never anticipated to emerge.

Even if you cannot get to kindness automatically at first, even if it is your second, reconsidered response, it means you are actively working towards your Soft Answer goal. We actively practice kindness, with the goal that it becomes part of our very fabric: completely reflexive (or as close to that as we can get). Stick with it and you will get there.

Be the First to Say Something Nice

There is an old saying: "If you can't say something nice about someone, don't say anything at all." A skill that may be even more challenging, and more useful, is to teach yourself to be able to honor everyone you meet by saying something positive to them.

When you see someone with whom you typically have a tough time, you do not need to wait for them to greet you first. Jump right in with a kind remark, and see what happens.

No matter how difficult it may seem, this is a skill you can actively cultivate. Greeting a habitual verbal aggressor with honor and kindness can be so unexpected that it can throw a potential verbal rant off its track before it even begins. We have known it to completely transform previously intractable relationships.

Everyone has some redeeming qualities. Think about how you can honor even the most difficult people. Can you find a way to commend or appreciate them? It can be small:

- *You're so prompt; I really value that.*
- *You're always focused on improving our work; I admire that quality.*
- *Thanks for hearing me out the other day; it really meant a lot to me.*

Do this enough, and it will become a habit, a completely reflexive habit of kindness that you do not even have to think about. It will just be there.

Exercises in Kindness

The more you apply yourself towards intentional kindness, the more you will develop habits of reflexive kindness. Here are some ways to help you practice and visualize intentional kindness:

Say Something Kind: Think of a person you have a lot of difficulty with or have very little regard for. What can you say that is kind about this person? ...to this person? What can you say that is positive about this person that you could say sincerely? Get prepared for the next time you meet, so you can say it like you really mean it. When that time comes, say your nice thing, then just smile and wait for the response.

For someone who likes to give you unsolicited advice:

- *You're always so resourceful and willing to help.*

For someone who tends to criticize your appearance:

- *You have a very artistic sensibility, and an ability to see a certain potential in me that I always miss.*

For someone who keeps arguing:

- *I appreciate that you really seem to want to get to the bottom of this. How can we move toward that?*

Be a Perfect Guest: Imagine you are a guest in the house, office or town of someone that you highly respect. How can you be a perfect guest here? How would you behave to show your reciprocal respect and appreciation?

Be a Seasoned Traveler: Imagine you are visiting a country with a culture very different from your own. In a country where you are not familiar with the customs, how would you determine what constitutes skillful kindness?

Be a Soft Answer Hero: Who are the Soft Answer heroes in your life and how do they handle difficult situations? You could keep a list of people you admire in the *Gratitude List* section of your Soft Answer notebook, and the skills of communication and diplomacy they use could be added to the *Favorite Strategies* section. Can you imagine yourself using one of these strategies in the future?

Once you get the hang of this, try something a little harder to do: when you are in the middle of a difficulty, try to get your new reflex of kindness to kick in.

~

REMEMBER THAT YOU CAN NEVER CHANGE ANOTHER PERSON, BUT YOU can change how you communicate and engage with them. Just this can open the door to new behavior options for both of you, which could make a bumpy start more manageable.

Equilibrium, just like life, is fluid and dynamic. You have to constantly be thinking on your feet. When you begin to realize that balance is not a static state, and that it requires vigilance, you continuously come up with actions to restore equilibrium. To the extent that these actions can come from a place of honor and kindness, you are avoiding the risk of reverting to habitual retorts. Retorts that come from fear are counter actions that throw you back into fight or flight mode.

When conversations break down, we look for solutions that can restore peace and balance, and which avoid sowing seeds for future conflict. Kindness is not about always saying "yes," nor being a pushover. Kindness has the potential to de-fuse and diffuse a situation so that no one loses.

Cultivating Forgiveness

Seek Out Forgiveness Stories: Start looking for and learning stories of forgiveness.

These can be true, fictional, in written form, or in podcast or documentary form. You may recall stories in your own life when you were unexpectedly, generously, forgiven, or when you were a witness to an extraordinary act of forgiveness.

As you read, listen to, and watch these stories, consider the mettle, courage, faith and generosity that forgiveness requires. (See links and other resources below to help you get started.)

Learn More About the Practice, and the New Science, of Forgiveness: It is beneficial for us to forgive. Forgiveness is the subject of cutting-edge research and is part of cultivating optimal health, both psycho-emotional and physical. See the resources below for a start on learning more about forgiveness.

See Yourself as a Valuable Part of the Unofficial Network of People Who Deliberately Extend and Spread Forgiveness: Forgiveness is not easy, but we are not in this alone! There is a growing global community of organizations and individuals who are actively cultivating the practice of forgiveness. We can work together to make forgiveness contagious.

Resources for Forgiveness Stories

The Forgiveness Project explores the possibilities of forgiveness through real stories: TheForgivenessProject.com

Fred Luskin of the *Stanford University Forgiveness Projects*, says, "Forgiveness is a trainable skill, just like learning to throw a baseball." *Forgive For Good* website and program teaches just this: LearningTo-Forgive.com

Picking Cotton: As a college student, Catherine Thompson was brutally attacked. In shock, confused, and influenced by a composite drawing created from her description of the perpetrator, she picked Ronald Cotton out of a lineup, and he was wrongfully convicted and imprisoned. Through DNA evidence years later, Cotton was found innocent and released. Thompson contacted him to apologize, only to learn that he had already forgiven her. What resulted was their book, *Picking Cotton*. Today, Thompson heads the *Healing Justice* organization, which helps wrongfully convicted people restore their lives. HealingJusticeProject.org PickingCottonBook.com

From *Reader's Digest*: "10 Inspiring Stories of Extreme Forgiveness": RD.com

Resources for the Science and Practice of Forgiveness

The International Forgiveness Institute arose out of research done at the *University of Wisconsin*, Madison. Their website offers a wealth of resources: InternationalForgiveness.com

The Mayo Clinic offers a compelling article on the impact of forgiveness, or the lack of it, on our health: MayoClinic.org

University of Colorado Conflict Information Consortium hosts a *Beyond Intractability and Conflict Resolution* knowledgebase: BeyondIntractability.org

The Fetzer Institute website has videos and other resources focusing on forgiveness, a key initiative for the organization: Fetzer.org

Pocket Cards: Reflexive Kindness; Forgive; Say Something Nice

PART VIII

HOME AGAIN

22

COMPASSION BEGINS AT HOME

You are the hero of your own story.

— JOSEPH CAMPBELL

You have to have confidence in your ability, and then be tough enough to follow through.

— ROSALYN CARTER

No matter how much training we do or how many meditation classes we attend, all of us can get overtired, whiny, scared, aggressive, despondent, pouty, and angry and irrational. We all have our moments of poor judgment...which just means we never stop being human.

That said, there is a lot we can to do to improve our self-management skills. We have created The Soft Answer system to help.

When we slip and not do or say as we were planning, or when we fall back into our old habits, this can be a good time to be gentle with ourselves, relax, breathe, and perhaps write in our Soft Answer notebooks.

It is important that at these times we do not (as Jack Kornfield says), "beat ourselves up for being human." Learn as much as possible from the inevitable backsliding, and capture as much value as you can from the experience. Notice what is happening at these times. What was your mood like before? What was the trigger? How long did your recovery take? How did your body feel? How hard is it to remember the details of the experience? How hard is it to set those memories aside? Remember: compassion begins at home.

Persevering

Often we are unaware of getting into trouble conversationally. It is no surprise that we run out of energy, become reactive rather than intentional, and end up exhibiting behavior we ultimately regret. One preventative measure we suggest is to cultivate purposeful perseverance, a spirited, determined confidence when the odds are against you or circumstances are difficult. It is behaving heroically and having courage: "You are the hero of your own story."

Take courage as you bring your new Soft Answer skills to the wider world. Remember that courage has at its root, the French word coeur: heart. Being purposeful requires a conscious energy state, in which we are rewiring our reflexes. This gives us the chance to have a better outcome when the situation gets overloaded.

The Soft Answer Verbal T'ai Chi system works. It works as a practice and an art, not as a magic bullet. If you get discouraged along the way and think, "I've tried it and it didn't work," it may help to remember your purpose of being a force for healthier interactions in the world.

A Soft Answer practice is more like a marathon than a sprint. You have to pace yourself. We keep the principles of the practice in mind, but we cannot expect instant mastery. Bear in mind that in any great endeavor, practice is essential, and progress is never linear.

To be able to sustain yourself and stay the course over the long run, be gentle with yourself, and be realistic. Everyone slips up, especially when they are trying something new and even more especially when trying to turn old, embedded habits around. Remember that compassion begins at home. Forgive yourself and move forward.

Train yourself to deliberately conduct yourself with purposeful perseverance. When you do, chances are you will hold your body differently and exude more confidence, your voice will sound clearer, people will respond more favorably and interactions will go more smoothly.

So Go Easy. Start in the small places. Look for the more relaxed moments in which you can engage the philosophy and apply the techniques naturally and comfortably.

Then, in the more stressful, larger moments, you may be surprised about what skills present themselves—perhaps even effort-lessly—as a natural byproduct of your practice.

Watch a Movie

Your Soft Answer heroes do not have to be real people. Try watching a movie that features a purposeful, persevering hero (like yourself!):

9-5
The Blind Side
Clueless
The Color Purple
Double Happiness
Erin Brockovich
Forrest Gump
Fried Green Tomatoes
Legally Blonde
Mulan
October Sky
Rabbit Proof Fence
Ratatouille
The Secret of Roan Innish
Sing Street
Steel Magnolias
Stuart Saves his Family

Whale Rider
What about Bob?

Forgive Yourself

Some may think that forgiveness is something we bestow upon others for some real or perceived grievance we have suffered, but all the benefits of forgiving also apply when we see fit to forgive ourselves.

If you are having a hard time letting go of the feeling that you have failed, and must carry the burden of this guilt until you can drag yourself to higher ground, then you have consigned yourself to a long uphill battle—with yourself.

One of the reasons that we may have trouble forgiving ourselves is that we are reluctant to support the illusion that we are now off the hook. We may think that forgiving ourselves will somehow allow us to forget the offending behavior. Remember, in forgiveness, we are not excusing the "failure"; we are letting go of the illusion that holding onto the mistake is what is keeping us from repeating it in the future.

Some of us may feel that not forgiving ourselves is a way of atoning for our past mistakes, but actually it is a symptom that we have not yet accepted them. This thinking keeps us stuck in place and makes it hard to move forward. If we really accept and take owner-ship of our mistakes, we should also be able to accept that we can forgive ourselves for them.

Forgiving ourselves makes it possible, and even more likely, to avoid repeating the same wrongdoings.

It is hard to let go. We often think we have forgiven someone, only to find ourselves revisiting old grievances. It may take many returns to forgiveness to finally let go. The same holds true when we move to forgive ourselves. It may be hard to know where to begin, because we may not be aware of our need for self-forgiveness.

Forgiving others allows us to move forward with our lives, but unless we forgive ourselves as well, we will keep ourselves from being able to embrace the good things yet to come.

Forgive yourself. It does a body good.

Pocket Cards: Compassion Begins at Home; Persevere; Be the Hero of Your Own Story; Start Small; Forgive Yourself and Move Forward

23

WE'RE IN THIS BOAT TOGETHER

We are all in the same boat, in a stormy sea, and we owe each other a terrible loyalty.

— G. K. CHESTERTON

Out beyond ideas of wrongdoing and rightdoing, there is a field. I'll meet you there.

— RUMI (TR. COLEMAN BARKS)

W e're all in this boat together, and our differences, challenging as they may be at times, allow us the opportunity to seek balance. Why not support and encourage one another as much as possible?

To keep our boat from capsizing, we need to maintain our balance and equilibrium. Balance and equilibrium are dynamic. They are fluid states. Trying to find a static or permanent state of balance, justice or fairness would be a misreading of what life is: justice and fairness are never guaranteed, and balance must be continually sought.

When something feels unfair, when someone seems wrong, when there's an unjust accusation, can we let go of all the "yes, buts" and return again to the basic framework of equilibrium and balance? This requires an ability to change, to move. One technique that can shift two people into a more favorable equilibrium is to move together.

Invite Someone to Move with You

When you ask someone to move with you, you are inviting them to join you towards a common purpose. It literally puts you both on the same side of something: they are on your side, and you are on theirs, at least in this small act. Even if it seems almost insignificant (getting some water or fetching your sweater in another room), the fact that the two of you are physically working towards a common goal can change your dynamic just enough to rebalance a situation.

Practice this first with a partner, and then try it when things are getting tough in a social situation: invite someone to move with you.

- *Can we walk into the next room for a minute? I need to get a glass of water.*
- *My legs feel a bit restless. Would you mind talking about this while we walk?*
- *I'm feeling a bit chilly. Would you mind continuing this conversation while I find where I left my jacket?*
- *I was just about to get some coffee. Do you want to come with me and we can talk about this on the way?*

Another advantage to asking someone to move with you is, if the other person is looking for a graceful way out of the situation, you have just given it to them. They now have the option to say, "No thanks, you go ahead. This discussion can wait; we'll talk later."

Remember: resolving conflict is never about getting even. As we have said before, the quest for getting even offers only cheap, short-term satisfaction that almost always sets up the next problem. Can we remember to *find the third option*?

Can we look beyond our differences to see the more fundamental connections that we each have with one another? Can we be generous, give people the benefit of the doubt, and offer encouragement?

Offer Encouragement

In the previous chapter, we addressed developing courage for ourselves; now we look at offering it to others. When you *en-courage* someone, you literally seek to instill them with courage. In doing so, you demonstrate that you are on their side. A few simple words of encouragement can deftly move a potentially negative dialogue in a new, more positive direction.

If we think a challenging conversation might be at hand, we can offer encouragement by jumping in before trouble has a chance to begin:

- *I'm glad I ran into you; I've been meaning to tell you I thought your ideas about the project were so original.*
- *Can I just say that you're doing a great job with the ...*

Sending out encouragement is like the ringing of a bell. A bell is tapped in one spot, but the reverberations are felt all over and produce a beautiful sound. A kind word goes a long way; people are much less likely to come down hard on someone who has just said something nice to them. Even if they need to pass along a complaint or a criticism, chances are, they will be kinder and more thoughtful about it if the conversation begins on a friendly note. This may increase your chances of resolving a problem together more quickly.

Both parties, feeling the success of this encounter, may be more likely to pass kind feelings on to the next person they meet. Here, the same dynamic that occurs in "kick the dog," creates a chain of positive energy instead. This string of kindhearted actions may directly benefit us and may extend further than we can know.

Another way to look at a healthy balanced world is to compare it to a healthy body. A body has many trillions of cells, ultimately forming the many components (organs, muscles, bones, etc.) that make up our body. These components may look different and perform different functions, but when they are healthy and work together, it is a beautiful thing. If any of these components behaves in an unhealthy way, it is in our best interest to return them to good health—to restore equilibrium—because the health of the whole body is reliant on the health of the individual cells.

Making it a point to be a person who spreads good health and stability helps to move our world in a positive direction. We may not see the effect of what we cause immediately, but we may someday benefit from the effect of what we or someone else has passed along. Seeing ourselves as being in the same boat as others and recognizing that benefitting others ultimately benefits us can make the other techniques we have presented in *The Soft Answer* easier to put into practice.

Pocket Cards: We're in this Boat Together; "Move with Me;" Use Kind Words; Offer Encouragement

24

RECIPES
(PUTTING IT ALL TOGETHER)

If you get, give. If you learn, teach.

— Maya Angelou

We awaken in others the same attitude of mind we hold toward them.

— Elbert Hubbard

In making the most of this program, we are counting on you to use these materials to build your own Soft Answer toolkit. We hope you take what works for you and leave what does not—you can always come back to something later.

How will you know which technique to use and when?

Just like with physical tools, when you first try to use them you may feel awkward or clumsy, but gradually you develop comfort and skill. Rest assured that Soft Answer tactics are designed to weave together synergistically over time. As you continue your Soft Answer practice, you will surely develop an intuition and an instinct that has experience and research-in-action behind it. You will be able to improvise, combine techniques, and maybe come up with your own new ones. (Please tell us about them!) Be patient with yourself, and give yourself permission to experiment and to stumble.

Your Soft Answer practice will be your own expression of the principles and philosophy we have shared, because this is an art— more like sculpting than following a static blueprint for a structure. This is the start of a Soft Answer technique. Ultimately you will make it your own. As with cooking, over time you create your own recipes as you apply your own experience, sensibility and style.

Imagine someone you know coming up to you suddenly, agitated and flustered, and talking a mile a minute. You do not know if this person is venting, upset with you, or even what the problem might be, as the person does not seem to be landing on any particular point. Here is just one way that the Verbal T'ai Chi process may play out:

• Tuning in to your whole body experience, you *Relax* (yet stay alert). Not wanting to be caught up in the tidal wave of emotion, you *Breathe* and stay *Low Drama*.

• Next, you note your own body language, keeping yourself grounded. You shift to one leg and turn just a little (*Open the Book*). Because the other person is at a high level of agitation, you move very slowly and carefully, but also with care and *compassion* toward the other person. You want to stay connected to the *person*, but distanced from their *agitation*.

• Then, you *Listen Deeply*. What is this person saying? Are they asking for help? Are they upset with you (for something reasonable or unreasonable)? Maybe it is hard to tell. You decide to ask a specific, "*Tell me more*" question: "Is the concern about _____, or is the concern about ____?" This question may help the other person find *Ground*. It has the potential to gently provide a focus for their agitation, and may put them back in the mode of problem solving. In asking this carefully crafted question, you indicate that you are listening, interested, attentive, and "with them."

• Next, you *Level* with the person, being honest and sincere. Understanding that you may or may not be the solution to this person's problem, you also know that, if this person has come to you with this issue, you have the potential to manage the interaction in a way that calms the situation down. You also know that, once the situation is a bit calmer, it will be easier to take the next step. Perhaps that next step is having an open, honest discussion about the problem. Perhaps the next step lies in opening a new direction for the problem to be solved.

Some people see recipes as strict instructions: no substitutions, no adjustments. Others look at recipes as general guidelines, and through experience and culinary intuition, know that it is reasonable to swap out an ingredient or adjust a method. The Soft Answer "recipe" listed above is specific to this situation. It has a measure of relaxation, a pinch of *Open the Book* ... and, it brings the whole scenario "off the boil." Every situation, every interaction, every pair of conversational partners is going to be just a little bit different. Finding that magic mix of ingredients and process will be up to you.

This work cannot be accomplished with a set of scripts. It is an individualized practice that you yourself develop. The techniques we offer are particularly helpful when you are new at this, or when you feel stuck or caught off guard. Ultimately, your Soft Answer practice should become as effortless and natural as the reflexive, possibly less helpful, set of responses you currently use as a personal coping prescription.

Attune to your own comfort level and stay within it. Allow your unique way of dealing with the world to be integrated with the philosophy. We know a Soft Answer practice is a creative act, and that each person working with it will have something valuable to share with others. It is a practice that can allow you to bring out the best in yourself while allowing others to bring out the best in themselves as well. Getting a set of new moves down, as in learning to dance, requires concentrated slow effort, but once you have internalized it, you get a flow on the dance floor that transcends any given lesson.

Pocket Card Jumble

You can use your Pocket Cards in training your reflexes to combine Soft Answer techniques in any number of ways. Go through your

Pocket Cards and randomly pull out two or three. Can you imagine a response that would combine them? What kind of scenario might call for such a response? This can be done individually or in a group.

In a group, you can lay a set of Pocket Cards face down on a table. One by one, each person turns three cards over, then tries to come up with a response that combines them all and tries it out on the group. What does everyone think?

Sharing Your Practice with Others

Behaviors are contagious. Negative behaviors such as bullying are learned behaviors. When someone is bullied they are more likely to try to bully others. People who live in an environment of rudeness are more likely to be rude themselves. They will also be more likely to perceive neutral comments as being rude.

Positive behaviors can be just as contagious. We want to spread calmness, joy and respect. With a Soft Answer practice, when verbal aggression comes our way, we may be able to render it futile. When an aggressor discovers that bullying behavior does not work with us, they will have to rethink their strategy if they want to communicate or hold our attention. When they try a more civil approach, we generously and graciously allow them the opportunity to succeed, and support their own awakening to the benefits of a Soft Answer practice.

Imagine this scenario multiplying outward. Even if only half of the people with whom we now have difficult relationships have a positive response to our Soft Answer Verbal T'ai Chi skills, this gives us a better quality of life. Now imagine that our new, more confident, more skillful behavior inspires others around us to learn what we have learned. How much more joyful and bright would their lives become? And, what about others in this ever-expanding network? How might their lives change when someone they once dreaded seeing becomes a more aware, compassionate, and grounded individual?

Trouble and hardness in life are unavoidable. This work is effective in preventing a large part of life's more avoidable difficulties. It has made a positive difference in our lives, and we hope you will be as motivated to share it with others as we are.

Just as compassion begins at home, peace also begins at home. Wage peace, both with yourself and others.

We wish you all the best.

Pocket Cards: Be Patient with Yourself; Stay at Your Comfort Level; Wage Peace

FINAL (AND NOT SO FINAL) THOUGHTS

Peace is possible.

— Mattie J.T. Stepanek

It took me quite a long time to develop a voice, and now that I have it, I am not going to be silent.

— Madeleine Albright

As we were finishing this book, we kept running into new things we felt very strongly needed to be included. (How can we NOT tell them about...?)

But then we also realized that if we stopped every time something new came up, the project would never be finished.

This book lays out a solid Soft Answer introduction, but it is not complete. How could it be? Humans have been interacting for thousands of years and there are endless permutations of these. New ones will continue to emerge.

Another reason this book can never be fully complete, is that one essential ingredient is missing: you and your own unique application of the techniques and principles we have been presenting. Without you, they stay in the book. With you, the system goes out into the world, and everyone around you begins to get a taste of it, and the goodwill can spread.

Even though The Soft Answer Verbal T'ai Chi system is still young, we have already heard from so many of you who have used it to turn a conversation, a work environment or a relationship around; and we are heartened and grateful. We are inspired by those of you who speak to us at workshops to say that you have returned a second time to deepen your understanding of the material. We're excited when we hear from those of you who have shared the material with others, and report that their lives have been changed for the better as well. We appreciate your stories of how you no longer dread going to work or to family events because of your newly acquired skills, or how a colleague or family member who once seemed menacing or intimidating has become a thoughtful and valued member of your community.

Consider taking yourself through this material again, possibly with different group. Every group is different, and there is a special synergy that emerges when groups work together with a common purpose.

Lastly, let us know if you have organized a group at your workplace, bookclub, or school. We are eager to learn how it is going (both the ups and the downs), and any new ideas you come up with along the way. You can reach us through the contact page on our website, TheSoftAnswer.com where you will also find the latest about what's happening and additional resources.

We look forward to hearing from you!

PART IX

APPENDIX

QUOTATIONS

POCKET CARDS

SOFT ANSWERS

QUOTATIONS

Quotations used in this book, in order of appearance

Never doubt that a small group of thoughtful, committed citizens can change the world.[^®]*Indeed, it is the only thing that ever has.*

— MARGARET MEAD, USED WITH PERMISSION

To win without fighting is best.

— SUN TZU

Anger, fear, aggression - the dark side of the force are they.

— YODA

There is no exercise better for the heart than reaching down and lifting people up.

— JOHN ANDREW HOLMES, JR.

If you want others to be happy, practice compassion. If you want to be happy, practice compassion.

— XIV DALAI LAMA

The most important thing in communication is hearing what isn't said.

— PETER DRUCKER

When you really pay attention, everything is your teacher.

— EZRA BAYDA

If you know the enemy and know yourself, you need not fear the result of a hundred battles.

— SUN TZU

The wise one breathes to the bottom of the heels.

— CHUANG TZU

I keep my ideals, because in spite of everything I still believe that people are really good at heart.

— ANNE FRANK

A mind is like a parachute. It doesn't work if it is not open.

— FRANK ZAPPA

Do what brings you joy, and your purpose will unfold.

— IYANLA VANZANT

Be sincere; be brief; be seated.

— FRANKLIN DELANO ROOSEVELT (BY WAY OF JAMES
ROOSEVELT, RECALLING HIS FATHER'S ADVICE ON THE ESSENCE
OF PUBLIC SPEAKING)

Joy is the skill of skills.

— SUZETTE HADEN ELGIN

Empty, empty. Happy, happy.

— AJAHN JUMNIEN

Sincerity is impossible, unless it pervade the whole being, and the pretense of it saps the very foundation of character.

— JAMES RUSSELL LOWELL

Truth is such a rare thing, it is delightful to tell it.

— EMILY DICKINSON

What you believe to be true is true, within certain limits, which are themselves beliefs.

— JOHN LILY

Whatever you feed will grow.

— SUZETTE HADEN ELGIN

Negative people need drama like oxygen. Stay positive, it will take their breath away.

— (Attributed to both) MJ Korvan and Tony Gaskins

Mind like water.

— Martial arts adage (Author unknown)

You grow up the day you have your first real laugh at yourself.

— Ethel Barrymore

Walk as if your feet are kissing the Earth.

— Thich Nhat Hanh

Our hearts resonate at the same frequency as the earth and the universe. Therefore, we are all valuable instruments in the orchestration of the world and its harmony.

— Suzy Kassem

Not the senses I have but what I do with them is my kingdom.

— Helen Keller

For fast acting relief, try slowing down.

— Lily Tomlin

The hurrier I go, the behinder I get.

— Grandmother Dixon's kitchen trivet

Go easy.

— RONALD T. LOWELL

I am not afraid of storms for I am learning how to sail my ship.

— LOUISA MAY ALCOTT

...give me grace to accept with serenity
the things that cannot be changed,
Courage to change the things
which should be changed,
and the Wisdom to distinguish
the one from the other.

— REINHOLD NIEBUHR

Every human being is entitled to courtesy and consideration.
Constructive criticism is not only to be expected but sought.

— MARGARET CHASE SMITH

Blame is not productive. Blame disguises and conceals. Blame
alienates and separates. Blame is the killer of community,
cooperation, and collaboration.

— PETER ROUSE

One thing moves, everything moves.

— T'AI CHI CLASSICS

You take your life in your own hands, and what happens? A terrible thing, no one to blame.

— Erica Jong

Defense is the beginning of war.

— James Dodd

We should strive, not only to say the right thing in the right place, but far more difficult, to leave unsaid the wrong thing at the tempting moment.

— Lady Dorothy Nevill

Don't Take the Bait.

— Suzette Haden Elgin

Against criticism a man can neither protest nor defend himself; he must act in spite of it, and then it will gradually yield to him.

— Johann Wolfgang von Goethe

Never explain—your friends do not need it and your enemies will not believe you anyway.

— Elbert Hubbard

Peace is not the absence of conflict, but the ability to cope with conflict by peaceful means.

— Ronald Wilson Reagan

When they go low, we go high.

— MICHELLE OBAMA

First seek to understand, then to be understood.

— ANONYMOUS

Spread love everywhere you go. Let no one ever come to you without leaving happier.

— MOTHER TERESA

When you're through changing, you're through.

— MARTHA STEWART

Live your life receptively, like a willow in the wind.

— THOMAS MOORE

Three things in human life are important. The first is to be kind. The second is to be kind. And the third is to be kind.

— HENRY JAMES

When you forgive, you heal your own anger and hurt and are able to let love lead again. It's like spring cleaning for your heart.

— MARCI SHIMOFF

You are the hero of your own story.

— JOSEPH CAMPBELL

You have to have confidence in your ability, and then be tough enough to follow through.

— Rosalyn Carter

We are all in the same boat, in a stormy sea, and we owe each other a terrible loyalty.

— G. K. Chesterton

Out beyond ideas of wrongdoing and rightdoing, there is a field. I'll meet you there.

— Rumi (tr. Coleman Barks)

If you get, give. If you learn, teach.

— Maya Angelou

We awaken in others the same attitude of mind we hold toward them.

— Elbert Hubbard

Peace is possible.

— Mattie J.T. Stepanek

It took me quite a long time to develop a voice, and now that I have it, I am not going to be silent.

— Madeleine Albright

POCKET CARDS

Ideas for pocket cards appear below listed in chapter order.

2. Find the Third Option

- Open the Book
- Find the Third Option

3. Compassionate Detachment

- Compassionate Detachment
- Stay Warm but Keep your Cool
- Create Space for Saving Face
- Saving Face: No Disgrace
- Think: "Poor thing. Desperate to communicate and that's the best she (or he) can do"
- Think: "Poor thing. Desperate for attention and that's the best he (or she) can do"

4. Pay Attention

- "Tell Me More"
- Pay Attention
- Listen Deeply

5. Relax and Listen Internally

- Relax
- Breathe
- Listen to Your Body
- Listen Internally
- Pay Attention to Your Breath
- Cultivate Relaxation
- Our relaxation is our protection

6. Start Fresh, Stay Open

- Start Fresh, Stay Open
- Don't Rush to Judgment
- Keep an Open Mind
- "Interesting..."
- Stick Lightly

7. Joy is the Skill of Skills

- Be Joyful
- Smile
- Levity and Brevity
- Whatever You Feed Will Grow

8. Be Sincere

- Say Something True
- Be Sincere

9. Low Drama

- Level
- Low Drama
- Be Direct
- Stay Centered and Neutral
- Be Boring

10. Ground

- Cultivate Humility
- Stay Grounded
- Ground
- Return to Your Center
- Breathe to the Bottom of Your Feet

11. Come to Your Senses

- Harmonize
- Connect
- Match a Sensory Mode
- Stay Neutral

12. Take Your Time

- Go Easy
- Take Your Time
- Buy Time
- Breathe
- Sl-o-o-o-w D-o-w-w-w-n

13. Boundaries

- Take Your Sails Out of Their Wind
- Take Responsibility
- Respect Healthy Boundaries
- Adjust and Keep Adjusting as Necessary
- My Stuff, Your Stuff
- "Yes, and ..."

14. Drama Triangles

- Low Drama
- Avoid Drama Triangles

15. Don't Kick the Dog!

- Don't Kick the Dog!
- Don't Play the Blame Game
- Solve Problems Together
- Suspend Judgment
- Be a Positive Influence
- Let it Go!

16. Don't Take the Bait!

- Locate the Bait
- Don't Take the Bait!
- "All of a sudden I found myself..."

17. Steer Clear of JADE

- Steer Clear of JADE
- Neutralize

18. Managing Sneak Attacks

- Be Kind, Rewind
- "Let's take a step back"
- Provide a graceful way out
- Use Platitudes

19. Both Sides Now

- Validate First
- Seek to Understand
- Apply Miller's Law
- Get Perspective

20. Reconfigure

- Reconfigure
- No Insistence, No Resistance
- Spring Back Up

- Readjust
- Stay Comfortable

21. Reflexive Kindness

- Reflexive Kindness
- Forgive
- Say Something Nice

22. Compassion Begins at Home

- Compassion Begins at Home
- Persevere
- Be the Hero of Your Own Story
- Start Small
- Forgive Yourself and Move Forward

23. We're in this Boat Together

- We're in this Boat Together
- "Move with Me"
- Use Kind Words
- Offer Encouragement

24. Recipes

- Be Patient with Yourself
- Stay at Your Comfort Level
- Wage Peace

SOFT ANSWERS

S oft Answers are delivered with sincerity and respect. We aim to stay connected while remaining grounded, centered and relaxed. Our goal is to restore balance, never to "best" anyone.

Different situations call for different strategies and techniques, but as you continue to work with The Soft Answer Verbal T'ai Chi, you will develop your own sense of what might work when.

Many Soft Answer responses fall into more than one strategic category, and obviously not all answers apply to all situations. The list below is intentionally broad and gives a general framework to support your personal Soft Answer journey.

Compassionate Detachment

- *That's got to be difficult.*
- *It sounds like you've got a lot going on right now.*
- *It can be so frustrating when you feel you're not being understood (listened to, respected, ...).*
- *Ask for more Information:*
- *Tell me more...*

- *Tell me more, if you don't mind.*
- *Hmmm...that never occurred to me...can you tell me more about that?*
- *Huh! I never would have thought about it that way. Please, go on.*
- *That's such an interesting perspective; can you talk a bit more about that?*
- *Would you mind expanding on the idea of ....? I'd really appreciate it.*
- *You wouldn't want to tell me a bit more about that, would you?*
- *How did you reach that conclusion?*
- *Is the concern about _____, or is the concern about ____?*

Stay Open

- *Interesting...*
- *I guess I never would have thought of that.*
- *That's a surprising (good, interesting, valid, unexpected, original, curious) question (point, perspective, angle on this, consideration)...*
- *I guess I'll have to think about it.*
- *Hmmmm...I wonder...*
- *Really? Well that's something...*
- *You're very possibly right on that point.*
- *What an interesting (unexpected, original, curious) thought.*
- *How did you reach that conclusion?*
- *Short and Sweet (Levity & Brevity):*
- *Thank You.*
- *I can't right now.*
- *No kidding.*

Say Something True

- *I have no doubt there are others who would agree with you.*
- *Wow, I guess I never looked at it that way...*
- *I hear what you're saying, I'm just not quite sure what it means.*
- *I know you did a lot of work and you put a huge amount of effort into making this a success. Thank you. (You are not saying that their efforts succeeded or were useful to the process. This person may have even been an obstacle. You are sincerely acknowledging the effort they made).*
- *I never really understood why people (...stayed there so long, etc.).*
- *It's hard for me to tell right now what I'll be doing next Thursday.*
- *That was a pretty crowded event.*
- *Lots of people lose their jobs unexpectedly.*
- *This is quite a party.*
- *There may be a lot of people who feel that way.*
- *Losing things can be very frustrating.*
- *I always like seeing people enjoying themselves.*

Level

- *It's an interesting perspective you have; I'm not sure I share it, though.*
- *I really didn't care for (that movie...etc.).*
- *That was not a very kind thing to say.*
- *I hear what you're saying, but I don't see that happening.*
- *Why, exactly, are you saying this to me?*
- *I don't believe I'm obliged to share that information with you.*
- *My personal information is just exactly that: personal.*
- *It feels like there's something here that I don't understand.*

- *Yes. I feel so good when I wear this.*
- *Aunt Rose gave this to me; I wanted her to see how much I'm enjoying it.*

Low Drama

- *You may be right.*
- *I get it.*
- *Oh.*
- *Boy.*
- *I can tell you've been thinking about this a lot.*
- *I hadn't thought about that.*
- *Yes, I am.*
- *My, you're the curious one today.*
- *I understand.*
- *I'm aware of that.*

Be a Little Dull

- *The processes people go through and the decision trees they use when they are trying to determine whether to attend various functions or participate in certain events on particular occasions can be completely mysterious, ...*
- *I completely understand why someone might be motivated to ask another person for their name, and I am quite sure that there are a number of people who would feel very comfortable giving their name out to perfect strangers, and maybe even their addresses...or perhaps they would agree to show an ID, like their driver's license or their passport, if they even carry one with them, because not everyone does, of course, but...*

Connect on a Sensory Level

- *I agree, you can't just close your eyes to that.*
- *I see.*
- *I hear you.*
- *You're coming in loud and clear.*
- *Let me just savor that for a moment.*
- *Let's walk through this together.*

Buy Time

You can Buy Time with just words, or by combining words with gestures or actions.

- *Well, you've certainly given me something to think about.*
- *Hmmm....I guess I'll have to think about that.*
- *It's obvious that this is important to you. Let's set aside a time when we can focus on it exclusively. (Respond this way only if you have some reasonable responsibility to do so.)*
- *Wow—that sounds interesting, but I'm not in a position to accept that kind of invitation right now.*

EXCUSE YOURSELF MOMENTARILY

- *I'm sorry. I drank a ton of coffee earlier and I really have to use the bathroom. I'll be right back.*
- *I really need to find a sip of water—would you excuse me for just a few moments?*

DROP SOMETHING EXPENDABLE (A NAPKIN, A PEN)

- Whoops! So clumsy of me! Now, where were we?
- Gosh, I seem to be all thumbs today! Oh, well. You were saying...?

- Ugh! Now I'm going to have to go find another fork. Please excuse me.

Clarify Boundaries

- I wouldn't know.
- I'm sorry, I can't help you with that.
- I just couldn't say.
- I have no idea.
- You have a really interesting way of looking at the world.
- You think of the most surprising things.
- That's a thought.
- Agree With What You Can:
- Yes, and...
- True, and also...
- Agreed, so maybe...
- Good point, and it leads me to wonder if...
- Yes, I see the problem.
- It's true that we haven't gone to the movies together in a very long time. It was great having that much free time.
- As you know...

Open Things Up

- Let's ask Mary. She's great at this stuff.
- This issue you raise is so important, I think it deserves the attention of everyone in the group. Why don't we add it to the agenda for our next meeting?

If Applicable, Own up

- You're right, I should have put the applesauce away before

I went to bed. I'm sorry about that. Now, what else is on your mind?

Neutralize

- Ah...
- Why does anyone ever...? I suppose there could be hundreds of answers to a question like that.
- I'm not sure how to answer that, but you're certainly pointing out something I hadn't thought of.
- That's quite a question.
- You have such an interesting mind. I'm not sure I'd ever think to ask a question like that.

Take a Step Back / Rewind

- Let's take a step back. I think you were saying that...
- Before we go on, can we go back to an earlier point you were making? I want to make sure I understand it correctly.
- Let's rewind for a second, may we? I'm interested in hearing more about...
- I think I need to take a step back to when you were talking about...

Use Platitudes

- Well, you win some. You lose some.
- Such is life.
- You never know.
- After a storm, the sun is bound to shine again.
- It's always darkest just before the dawn.

- Time will tell.
- Tomorrow is another day.
- Well, it is what it is.
- They are who they are.

Validate First

- Are you saying...
- I'm glad you brought that up, because I really think it's a critical point. And what goes right along with it, from my perspective, is...

Say Something Nice

- You're so prompt; I really value that.
- You're always focused on improving our work; I admire that quality.
- Thanks for hearing me out on this; it really means a lot to me.
- You're so resourceful and willing to help.
- You have a very artistic sensibility, and an ability to see a certain potential in me that I always miss.
- I appreciate that you really seem to want to get to the bottom of this. How can we move toward that?

Offer Encouragement

- That's unfortunate; but I guess if anybody can figure it out, you can.
- I'm glad I ran into you; I've been meaning to tell you I thought your ideas about the project were so original.
- Can I just say that you're doing a great job with the ...

- Invite Them to Move With You:
- Can we walk into the next room for a minute? I need to get a glass of water.
- My legs feel a bit restless. Would you mind talking about this while we walk?
- I'm feeling a bit chilly. Would you mind continuing this conversation while I find where I left my jacket?
- I was just about to get some coffee. Do you want to come with me and we can talk about this on the way?

Made in the USA
Columbia, SC
07 March 2020